Beholding His Face,

Your Face,

and the Face of Others

THE
FOUR
FACES
OF GOD

BEHOLDING HIS FACE, YOUR FACE, AND THE FACE OF OTHERS

Daniel Prior

To those who helped me learn...

To those who are learning...

CONTENTS

1 | INTRODUCTION

4 | CHAPTER 1 God's Face

11 | CHAPTER 2 Your Face

23 | CHAPTER 3 Maturity

37 | CHAPTER 4 The Heavenly Face Lift

45 | CHAPTER 5 The Four Faces of God

53 | CHAPTER 6 Introduction to the Layout of the Four Faces

61 | CHAPTER 7 The Lion

83 | CHAPTER 8 The Ox

99 | CHAPTER 9 The Man

113 | CHAPTER 10 The Eagle

127 | CHAPTER 11 The Four Faces in Leadership

135 | CHAPTER 12 Have a Face, Get a Face

139 | CONCLUSION

141 | ACKNOWLEDGEMENTS

INTRODUCTION

T his book comes out of my journey of relationship with God and friends that God brought into my life. I have sinned and fallen short of the glory of God. Life is a journey of restoration. Relationship with God and others is the means of restoration. This book is not a declaration of completion but an encouragement to press on. As I have walked the road of relationship with God and three men that God brought into my life, I have experienced and partaken of restoration. The Lord gave me a mentor in Don Crossland and true brothers to walk with. The journey is not over. This book is fruit from that journey.

In the beginning, man lost relationship with God and his place of home. Adam and Eve were driven from the garden that God planted for them to cultivate and be fruitful and multiply. In their sin, they had fallen from God's desire and intent, but they also put themselves in a position of solidifying their action forever. If they had eaten from the tree of life in their fallen state, they would have been stuck forever. So, God acted.

"And the Lord God said, Behold, the man is become as one of us, to know good and evil: and now, lest he put forth his hand, and take also of the tree of life, and eat, and live forever: Therefore, the Lord God sent him forth from the garden of Eden, to till the ground from whence he was taken. So he drove out the man; and he placed at the east of the garden of Eden Cherubims, and a flaming sword which turned every way, to keep the way of the tree of life." (Genesis 3:22-24 KJV)

God protected man from himself in his fallen state and set cherubim and a flaming sword to keep or guard the way of the Tree of Life. The cherubim and sword do not guard the tree of life they guard the way of the Tree of Life. There is a journey, process or, dare I say, a relationship that must be faced to eat of the tree of life.

This book walks through what I have learned as a disciple, a follower of Jesus. It starts with first things first. The first thing is the face of God. Then follows our face, the importance of maturity, and how our face is transformed. The book then focuses on the four specific faces of God that are revealed in the person of Jesus Christ through the four gospels with each gospel as a basis of seeing God's face. The material is not presented as canonized information but as a foundation for the reader to continue their journey of relationship with God and others.

Before we begin, we need to deal with a barrier you may have. The barrier is Exodus 33:20 "And he said, Thou canst not see my face: for there shall no man see me, and live" (KJV). There is an awareness in all of us that feels this reality. If we are honest with ourselves there is a part of us that knows to see the face of God would be beyond what we can control. This links back to the beginning of the human story when Adam and Eve hid themselves from the presence (face) of God in the garden. In Exodus, Moses did not ask to see God's face. Moses asked to see God's glory, which is an important distinction because revealing God's glory is connected to God's face. The context of this scripture is that Moses and the people were at Mount Horeb where they stripped themselves of their ornaments. God told Moses about going into the promised land. Moses was in the tent that he pitched outside of the camp. In verse 11 of chapter 33 it reads that, "the Lord used to speak to Moses face to face, just as a man speaks to his friend", so there must be more going on than the closure of the possibility that man can see the face of God. Moses appealed to God based on the favor he found in God's sight and God had told Moses in verse 14 of the same chapter that "My presence shall go with you, and I will give you rest." This word for presence in this verse is the same Hebrew word for face. So how does God say that His *paniym* (presence, face) will go before them and that the Lord used to speak *paniym* to *paniym*? There is more to this than what is written. Please allow yourself to put any barrier aside as we pursue further the idea of God's face and being able to have a face-to-face relationship with Him. There is a lot more to the story than a picked verse that would limit God's desire for us.

The purpose of this information is not to only build your database of information. This is for you to engage the face of God and be transformed as you walk out your relationship with God. It is challenging, humbling, and a great adventure to live and have life. Like a mine with many shafts or a river with many tributaries there is a lot to be explored. Take it slow, meditate and wonder in the riches of God's glory, as you see His face, your face, and the face of others.

CHAPTER 1

GOD'S FACE

G od has a face. Do you? God desires to have face to face relationships. Do you? God is willing and has decided to let us see His face. What does this mean? Can we even see the face of God? What is a face? There is something about a face that is mystical, transformative, informative, relational, terrifying, and freeing. To behold someone, face to face is one of the most profound things in life. God has designed and created us to have a face because He fashioned us in His image.

The Hebrew word *paniym* is used over 2000 times in Scripture. As a masculine noun, it means face, presence, person, or surface. It is also used as an adverb and preposition, being translated as before or because of. Another key to this word is that it is plural but always used in a singular form. This speaks to some of the mystery of a face. It is a singular face but also plural. We will see that God's face is a singular face but also a plural reality.

God's face. Where does one begin? How can we speak

of God's face? God is beyond our thought, ways, and ideas. God is so great, eternal, omnipotent, omniscient, omnipresent. God is also the one who reveals Himself to us. Let us look at some of the scriptures that will help us to learn to see God's face.

The Lord tells Moses to tell Aaron and his sons how they should bless the sons of Israel. The blessing is this: "The Lord bless you and keep you; The Lord make His face shine upon you and be gracious to you; The Lord lift up His countenance on you and give you peace" (Numbers 6:24-26 NASB). Then Aaron and his sons are told "So they shall invoke My name on the sons of Israel, and I then will bless them." The name of the Lord and the blessing of the Lord for the sons of Israel is based on the face of the Lord. The face of the Lord is tied to His blessing, keeping, graciousness, and peace. That is amazing. The Lord making His face shine on the people releases the grace of the Lord on them. The Lord lifting up His countenance on the people leads to them receiving peace. The intent of God is for His people to know His face, to see it, and to be blessed beyond their comprehension of it.

Next, let us look at some verses in the Psalms. David says in Psalm 16:11 "Thou wilt shew me the path of life: in thy presence is fulness of joy; at thy right hand there are pleasures for evermore." (KJV) The word presence is *paniym*. In the face of the Lord, there is fullness of joy. To see the face of God and be in His face is fullness of joy. God allows us in the place of relationship to know what it means to have fullness of joy. This also would show that our lack of joy could be connected to the fact that we are not looking and residing in the face of our Lord. In Psalm 21:6 David writes, "For Thou makest him blessings forever, Thou dost cause him to rejoice with joy, By Thy countenance" (YLT). Once again, the Lord makes him rejoice with joy because of His face. Psalm 143:7 reads, "Hear me speedily, O Lord: my spirit faileth: hide not thy face from me, lest I be like unto them that go down into the pit" (KJV). David recognizes that the face of the Lord being hidden from him is terrible for him. It is a matter of life and death. Without the Lord's face he would be like those who go down to the pit. The face of the Lord saves us; it protects our life from descending into the pit. There is power in the face of the Lord that delivers us from living life in the pit. One more scripture from Solomon, in Proverbs 16:15, "In the light of a king's face is life, And his favor is like a cloud with the spring rain" (NASB 1995). The Lord is the King of kings. His face shines with light greater than the sun shining in its strength (Rev. 1). In His face is life, for He is life.

It is no wonder why we are told in Psalm 105:4 "Seek the Lord, and his strength: seek his face evermore." (KJV) Our life is dependent on the face of the Lord. It is His face that we are to seek. Without the face of the Lord, we cannot receive the life and light God desires for us to have, along with blessings, benefits, direction, purpose, etc. The Lord intends for us to have a face and to know that as He is, so are we in this world. The communication of the Lord is seen, heard, expressed, and felt in His face. The Lord has chosen to show us His face and for it to be toward us and rise upon us. Throughout history, He has been revealing His face.

God made the ultimate decision to let His face be known to us by incarnating Himself in the person of Jesus Christ. In the face of Jesus, we see the face of God.

The truth about God's face is that it is singular but also plural, so we have the story from not just one person but four that reveal His face. Part of the beauty of God is that His story and His face cannot be told or expressed by just one person. So how does God solve this wonderful problem? He decides to reveal Himself, in the flesh, in the person of Jesus and then also in our faces as we behold His face. Consider 2 Corinthians 4:6, "For God, who commanded the light to shine out of darkness, hath shined in our hearts, to give the light of the knowledge of the glory of God in the face of Jesus Christ." (KJV) His face, our face, in relationship beholding each other is the plan.

The reason we have the four gospels is because His face is seen through more than just one account. The four gospels show forth the four faces of God. The faces are the lion, ox, man, and eagle. These faces express His nature, identity, purpose, destiny, desire, glory, thoughts, ways, acts, love, and person. We are going to look at each of these faces in more detail so that we can see Him, His face, and be transformed to have a face like His. The Lord wants us to know His face, face His face, and to know our face so that our face will be like His.

Another unique scripture we find of God's face is in Matthew 18:10, "Take heed that ye despise not one of these little ones; for I say unto you, That in heaven their angels do always behold the face of my Father which is in heaven." (KJV) What does this mean and why would Jesus say it? The context of this verse is Jesus speaking on who is the greatest in and entering the kingdom. He uses children as an example of how the kingdom works. Then He makes a statement about their angels.

I have wondered about those angels and what exactly they do and more importantly why they are doing it. It is a serious thing to offend the little ones. Jesus says it would be better for that person to have a millstone hung around his neck and thrown into the sea. The ministry of angels is to and for the heirs of salvation according to Hebrews 1:14, "Are they not all ministering spirits, sent forth to minister for them who shall be heirs of salvation?" These angels that behold the face of the Father minister to the children. God has created them to behold His face and then minister to the children, His face. This is how much God loves us in action. These angels minister to the children, the face of God. This is a preparatory work in their lives for the destiny and fullness of identity that God desires for them. This ministry of our angels plays a role in our development and maturity. The children are being ministered by their angels that behold the face of the Father. I am not entirely sure how their ministry happens, but the fact that Jesus gives a strong warning to those who offend the little ones shows that it is a serious dynamic not to be messed with in the kingdom. Although Jesus does not explain the Fathers face, it is evident that God is not trying to hide His face from His creation.

While God's face in its fullness might be beyond our grasping, He wants us to see it. He wants us to see His glory, character, life, love, substance, light, joy, peace, and all that He is. A face is much more than physical attributes. A face is the expression of being and identity. God wants us to know His very being.

CHAPTER 2
YOUR FACE

The face, what an interesting concept. What would life be like if we didn't have a face? How would we communicate? Do we create our own face? How much of the story of our life is written on our face? In communicating our lives and stories our face is the keystone of expression and revelation. In our confusion and deception, we have grown to think that the masking of our face is possible and even a good long-term plan. Our faces have a way of revealing the things that we think are hidden in the deep recesses of our being. The links that we will go to alter our face in trying to maintain its youth, symmetry, glow or whatever the word we use to describe it, reveals the deep importance we know that it holds in life. We all know the importance of our face and often the importance of covering it when we have something to hide. Our face identifies us more than any other part of our body. There is a reason that law enforcement takes a picture of our face for their records. There is a reason that the basis of identification paperwork is a picture. The pictures we post online and pass down through generations always show our face. Our face is an identifiable memory of our life and certain points in our life. Our face is the putting forth of our being and identity.

Our face is not only the place where we communicate emotion, intent, desire and articulate our breath into speech, but it is also the place that we receive. Using our face, we receive through hearing, seeing, tasting, touching, and smelling. All our senses are concentrated in our face. It is no wonder why our face is the place that is most impacted and responsive to the realities we face in life or not face in life – no pun intended. Our face expresses the "yes" and "no" answers that we process life by and some of the funniest faces when we are stuck in the uncertainty between "yes" or "no".

One of the coolest things I witness about people's faces is when I am ministering to someone who has had a failure of some sort. I was taught to pay attention to the person's face as they share their story. This is a simple concept, yet vital to healing and relationships. In one way it is basic human respect to look people in the eye when they share and especially when they are sharing their story and the intimate details of their shame, guilt, trauma, fears, or pain. What I notice is that, as someone shares their struggles, they always look away. They look down to the left or right and sometimes close their eyes. There is an avoidance of eye contact, but the avoidance is more than just eye contact. This dynamic is what I call face contact. There was an avoidance of having a face-to-face relationship. It played out like this: a person would come in and the session starts by allowing them to tell their story and what is happening in their life. As they share, they tend to look around and see how the faces of those who were listening respond.

This reaction was a person reading the response of the face. As they share, they usually come to a place where there is tremendous shame, guilt, pain, embarrassment, or trauma. When they hit that point, the tendency is for them to look away or shut their eyes. When they look away it is always easier to share the negative things. These negative things usually are translated in themselves to their identity. The expressions being something to the degree of "I am a horrible person," "I will never recover from this," "I will never be good enough," "I am less than human," "I am so stupid." At this point, we could challenge their statements using our face. The two scriptures that reveal the challenge are 1 Corinthians 13:12 and 2 Corinthians 3:18.

"For now we see through a glass darkly; but then face to face: now I know in part; but then shall I know even as also I am known." "But we all, with open face beholding as in a glass the glory of the Lord, are changed into the same image from glory to glory, even as by the Spirit of the Lord." (KJV)

The first scripture is in the context of love, which is called the love chapter of the Bible. The context of the partiality of our vision is because we do not see face-to-face. This points to the fact that our love is incomplete when we are not having a face-to-face relationship. The second scripture is the context of Moses coming down out of the mountain, after His encounter with God face to face, and covering his face before Israel. There is a veil that lies over the face and over the heart, but the veil is taken away in Christ. The principal in verse 18 is the reflective principle of God. With an open face, we behold in a glass (mirror) and are transformed into what we are seeing. As people created in the image of

God, our face functions in the same way to others that behold our face. Remember that to look into a mirror is to see yourself. So, we challenge the person to try to look into our face and see if they could repeat the negative things that they would claim as their identity. As they would look at us in the face, we would reflect to them not the fallen identity of who they thought they were but the identity of who Christ says they are. The result without fail is that they could never repeat what they had spoken of themselves without looking away and breaking facial contact.

You already know the power of your face in many ways but don't pay attention to it enough. Think of how we correct children with our facial expressions. We have sayings in our culture that directly reveal this importance. I know that growing up when I was in trouble or in a serious situation my mom would tell me to look her in the eye and then ask, "Do you understand me?". This probably has happened to you at some point and in some way. I remember people challenging each other with the phrase, "I bet you won't say it to my face." How many books have been written about how communication that happens behind someone's back damages and creates all kinds of problems? The political culture is always ablaze with things that happen behind closed doors, in secretiveness, with people refusing to face one another. The extreme tension and world of lies run rampant when we aren't faced with the face of those we speak against or contrary to. We judge and make life decisions based on people's face. I recently saw a video that pointed out that most successful salesmen and politicians do not have facial hair because being clean-shaven produces an image that is more trustworthy.

Every morning you do something to prepare your face for the day, yourself, and those who will see you. There are whole industries that have been created for our face. The American Academy of Facial Plastic and Reconstructive Surgery estimated that there were 1.4 million procedures done in 2021. In a lot of ways, marketing is about creating, handling and presenting faces so that desired outcomes happen. Intuitively, we know that the face is vital to human relationships and the fabric of civilization.

When one of my nephews was young, there was something I experienced that fascinated me. At the time, my nephew was around ten years old and he was wild. He grew up as the youngest of three boys. As the youngest, you learn to sometimes be the craziest or toughest so that you can compete and gain the respect of your older siblings. My nephews were over at my house, and we were all playing and roughhousing. Then something happened: my youngest nephew was running around, and he tripped or hit something and fell. When he fell, he hit his head very hard. When he hit, we all knew that it had to hurt, but he popped up and was fine. We asked if he was okay and brushed him off saying, "you're okay, just a little bump no problem." He seemed to agree that he was okay. He acted tough, and he was fine. The thing was that when his mom found out, after going upstairs, she was obviously concerned and expressed some frustration at the roughhousing. When he saw that her face was not communicating that he was okay and that it was no big deal, he began to cry and feel the pain of the fall. I thought this was interesting because I recognized that part of his pain, regret and expression was caused by the expression on the face of his mom. He had begun to cry and almost be distraught about what had happened. We had all thought that he was okay, and he thought he was okay until the face of someone else communicated a different message. We were a little taken back by the change in his reaction to the fall because we got in trouble and were confused at the dynamic change. I always remembered this because there was power in his mom's face that directly impacted his emotion, actions, and belief of the situation. This wouldn't be the only time I saw this dynamic play out with kids and the person or people in authority. There is power in the face of parents and those who have positions of authority. The power of the face is seen in the dynamics of every relationship, but what will they see if we don't have a face?

To talk about our face, we must talk about the reality of masks. It would be disingenuous to act like we show our true face most of the time. The pressure of the world and the deception that fills every corner of the world has twisted us away from the true beauty of God's creation and design. The problem is that, in God giving men power, man has taken that power and produced death, façade, hiddenness, and schemes of the world in an attempt to redeem their identity through themselves. However, man did have some help from evil actors and was deceived into compounding evil. Masks are the human expertise in our shame, guilt, sin, and iniquity. Have you ever been to a masquerade party? Are you aware you live in a masquerade world? Think about some of the masks that you wear or have worn. In masks, there is a draw of mystery. In one way the mystery of masks is good, but knowing the person under the mask is far better. Knowing the person for who they are is a scary thing to face because it presents us with the reckoning of individual sovereignty. To face a sovereign being is both the wild adventure of life and the harrowing journey of the unknown.

A mask is a covering that is used to conceal identity. From concealing identity, there flows a next step of creating a false identity that is placed on the mask so that it is no longer about concealing only but deceiving and leading in another direction. There are three categories of those who wear masks. These categories are the young, the naïve, and the wicked. These are also the progressions that we go through from concealment to deception. The space between concealment and deception plays out in a pretend or exploratory trial and error.

The young wear masks for reasons that may be legitimate or illegitimate. The young are those that have not grown. Having a face requires growth, discovery, adventure, choices, and an identity of meaning, and this doesn't happen overnight. The young, in their limited existence, are not held to the standard of those who are supposed to be mature. The masks of the young usually come from the identities of those who are around them or influence them. The face of the young is one of potentiality. That potential is a big deal and has value. In the lack of growth and development, the young create masks for protection, exploration of what their face could be, and discovery of relational dynamics. When we look at children the example of this idea is plenty. The immaturity of children is not something that we punish them for, but we do hold them to an expectation of growth. This expectation of growth is measured in learning and a willing desire to learn. This is what the young need to do in their life and in developing their face. They need to learn and have a willing desire to learn. Some of the young are not children, and as adults, we can be considered a youth. We can be the young in new fields of life. When we start a new job or travel to a new country, we are in a position of someone who is a novice in that new world and must learn what our face is in that world. When I traveled to Brazil for the first time and visited the favelas of Sao Paulo, I found myself immature in their world. I didn't really have a face that had grown in that world. I brought my American face and masks with me, but I found out that I had some growing and learning to do. So, after my time there and a willingness to learn, I started to develop more of my identity and didn't have to wear a mask of strength pretending to know what their culture was. The young wears masks for illegitimate reasons when they are unwilling to learn and want to remain in the position of immaturity. This idea quickly leads to the next group.

The naïve are those that wear masks because of their refusal to face the reality of choice. Everyone must make choices and a denial to make them puts us into the world of fantasy and pretending. Fantasy and pretending are not bad within themselves. They can be very helpful when used in the proper context of learning and developing possibilities. All growth requires making choices, some made by us, and some imposed on us. The naïve have become stuck in the place of refusing to look at the real issue that is faced and what choices should be made. The naïve have shirked the choice of life or death. Not facing the choice, the naïve become floaters in a reality that doesn't face the reality that is in front of them. "Beating around the bush" and "they talk the talk but don't walk the walk" are phrases that are pointing out that stuck place of pretend and fantasy. Masks are vital if you are naïve because they deflect the choice to other things, people, times, places, or any plausible option. There is great risk in facing the choice of life and death and we can easily get caught in the deception of delay. Being naïve may seem like a good option for reprieve but the bill always comes due. The choice of life and death must be faced. Being naïve long enough leads you into the third group of those who wear masks.

The progression from the masks of the naïve then flows into the masks of the wicked. The wicked, in general terms, are those that pursue themselves, their lives and their world as God. In this pursuit as God, they will ultimately put themselves in the position as God in others' lives and worlds. Wickedness is seen in five ultimate characteristics or drives. These drives are the "I will" statements found in Isaiah 14:13-14, "But you said in your heart, 'I will ascend to heaven; I will raise my throne above the stars of God, And I will sit on the mount of assembly In the recesses of the north. I will ascend above the heights of the clouds; I will make myself like the Most High'" (NASB). These "I will" statements are said in the heart. What is said in the heart is the starting place for the creation of our masks. These five "I will" statements flesh out to be self-righteousness, self-exaltation, self-appointment, self-display, and self-sustaining in that order. The wicked have gone through the progression of immaturity into naiveite and have arrived at the place where they make decisions to be self-identifying as god themselves. The masks of the wicked are formed to not only conceal the identity of the person and their heart but also to control, deceive and manipulate others. The masks become a vessel of a false image that is taken on as an identity of the wearer. Often it is the masks of the wicked that look the most perfect because the stakes are higher. There is a demand for a perfect image of a lesser identity among the wicked who are building and supporting their own identity and world.

The three groups of those who wear masks have their reasons but no matter how good your mask is it can never be your face. A mask may help you to learn what a face is or could be, but it is no different than a sign along the road that points to a destination. The sign may be colorful and attractive, but it will never be the fullness of the actual thing. The young use masks to conceal the lack of a face while they are growing. The naïve use masks to conceal their face from the choice of life and death. The wicked use masks in pride to conceal their face and control what they think they can through deception. You always have to live with your face or lack of a face. Our face will have to face life or death, for even God himself faces this choice. We should never allow the coverup to become the story or think that it is the ultimate issue. This is an easy trap we fall into today. We find ourselves arguing over the masks that we wear instead of having a face-to-face relationship. This is part of the trap and deception of masks. They will never let us face what is there. You have a face, and you probably have some masks that you have learned to wear in life. If there is any hope for having genuine relationships, it begins with the voluntary decision to show our face. This is a courageous choice that we make, or we face the day when our masks fail, and we find ourselves to be a deceiver.

The choice to live in a way that is honest and courageous allows us to have a face that shines forth giving light and life to ourselves and all that we encounter. God has called us to be kings and priests. Proverbs 16:15 tells us, "In the light of a king's face is life, And his favor is like a cloud with the spring rain." We aren't to cover our face with a mask. We are to allow our face to shine forth, revealing life to those that come into our domain. Our face is to radiate who we are and not be covered by a mask. Your face is more meaningful and valuable than you probably have considered. Don't underestimate your face. Your identity in Christ as a son of God, king, priest, father, mother, son, daughter, farmer, builder, creator, artist, athlete, writer, or soldier is important in the fullness of God's kingdom coming and His will being done.

CHAPTER 3
MATURITY

What does it mean to be mature? In one sense maturity is reaching a certain point of growth that we have established as adequate for independence. This could be a fruit that has grown enough to be separated from the parent plant. In life, it is much more difficult to define the point of maturity. In the lives of humans, it is better to define maturity in terms of capability, character, responsibility, and accountability. I haven't met anyone that has openly confessed that they don't want to be mature. I have met a lot of people that confess a desire to grow and be mature but have not grown or made the choice to face life in a way that develops maturity, including myself. It is a hard thing to acknowledge our immaturity and embrace the harsh reality of what maturity asks of us. The writer of Hebrews shares some strong words for us regarding discipline.

"You have not yet resisted to the point of shedding blood in your striving against sin; and you have forgotten the exhortation which is addressed to you as sons, "My son, do not regard lightly the discipline of the Lord, Nor faint when you are punished by Him; For whom the Lord loves He disciplines, And He punishes every son whom He accepts." It is for discipline that you endure; God deals with you as with sons; for what son is there whom his father does not discipline? But if you are without discipline, of which all have become partakers, then you are illegitimate children and not sons. Furthermore, we had earthly fathers to discipline us, and we respected them; shall we not much more be subject to the Father of spirits, and live? For they disciplined us for a short time as seemed best to them, but He disciplines us for our good, so that we may share His holiness. For the moment, all discipline seems not to be pleasant, but painful; yet to those who have been trained by it, afterward it yields the peaceful fruit of righteousness" Hebrew 12:4-11 (NASB).

The process of maturing according to God's image requires a voluntary acknowledgement of its need and a desire to participate in it. The writer says that in striving against sin we haven't resisted to the point that we shed blood. To sin is to miss the mark, generally, and to shed blood would be to reach the point where we give up our life so that the ultimate can be attained. When we recognize that we are lacking maturity, when we have missed the mark and have not voluntarily accepted the challenge to reach that maturity, we are to remember and take seriously, the discipline of the Lord. The love of the Lord is always connected to His discipline. This is to say that for there to be love there will be discipline. This is because the love of the Lord desires the best for us as His sons and discipline is the way from immaturity to maturity. The crux of the process lies in the phrase, "But if you are without discipline, of which all have become partakers, then you are illegitimate children and not sons." This is the choice that discipline asks. Do we receive discipline or reject it? Our answer to this determines our decision to be a son or make ourselves a bastard. All have become partakers by default. All of us face the choice.

The choice of receiving the discipline of the Father that loves us does not determine our actual pedigree. We have power in determining how our relationship with our Father functions and flourishes. When I was a child there were times that I would get mad at my parents, and in my anger and pain would claim that they did not love me or that I was not their child. I remember telling someone once that my dad had helped conceive me but that he wasn't my dad. I said this in my pain of not having him in my life growing up in the ways that I thought he should be there and that I wanted him there. My claims could never change the fact that my dad was my dad, but my choices could tremendously impact any relationship I could have with him. This is the same thing with our heavenly Father. If we reject His discipline, it does not mean that we are not born of Him. It means that we have put ourselves in the position of not having a relationship with him and we make our own identity to be not of Him. This means that we are rejecting Him and our relationship with Him.

What is discipline? Discipline is training, education, to correct mistakes and curb passions. In the scripture in Hebrews, those who receive it not only receive the love of the Father but also will produce the peaceful fruit of righteousness. So, you could define discipline as a trainer that yields a peaceful fruit of righteousness. Discipline takes legitimate passions, strengths, power, zeal, desires, needs, wants, and trains them to yield a specific result. The result is not necessarily a specific thing but a totality of oneness with God. The peaceful fruit of righteousness is the standard of God that harmonizes and reconciles all included parts in their proper place. Discipline helps us to have the legitimate things of life in legitimate ways. The problem that we have as humans is using legitimate things in illegitimate ways. Discipline is a trainer that changes this broken way of living into living that begets life. Discipline increases our capability, character, responsibility, and accountability. In this increase, we find that we grow from being children into sons reaching the maturity that God has planned for us. It is from this point that we are able to go forth and fulfill the calling and destiny of our lives.

The story of Eli and his sons in 1 Samuel 2:12-36 illustrates the serious consequences of using legitimate things in illegitimate ways and rejecting discipline. The sons of Eli were priests, but it describes them as sons of Belial, which means that they were worthless and wicked. They decided for themselves to use their legitimate position in an illegitimate way, forcing the people who brought their sacrifice to give it to them according to their own way. Eli heard of what they were doing and rebuked them. It says in verse 25 that they would not listen to the voice of their father. A prophet of the Lord confronts Eli for his wrongdoing and honoring his sons above the Lord. Then the prophet that confronts Eli tells him that there will not be an old man in his house and that the increase of his house will die in the prime of life. This reality of no old men in the house and his sons dying in the prime of their life were a result of not receiving the discipline of the Lord. When we don't receive discipline, not only will there not be any wisdom of tradition in our lives, but our offspring will die in the prime of life. The reason that the youth will die in their prime is because there are no old men in the house and the immaturity of the youth progresses into wickedness that produces death in their lives also.

There are many scriptures that speak of maturity, its importance and that we should mature, but let's look at the importance of our face and the face that we look at in the process of becoming and being mature. Our faces play a role in our maturing process, and it reveals the level of maturity that we walk in. Cain is the first example we will look at. In Genesis 4:1-15 we find the story of Cain and his brother Abel. Cain was the older brother of Abel and a tiller of the ground. Cain brought an offering from the fruit of the ground to the Lord and He had no regard for it. It says that Cain became very angry, and his countenance fell. The Lord asked Cain why he was angry and why his countenance had fallen. Why the questions? These questions illuminate that God did not think that Cain should be angry or allow his countenance to fall. The questions do illuminate two important questions in our maturing process. Cain was mature enough to bring an offering to the Lord, and he was mature enough to stand on his own before the Lord. In Cain's maturity and growth, he is now facing the reality of the Lord not regarding his offering. The two questions are markers of maturity and what we face in the maturing process. The Lord doesn't ask us questions as a way to condemn us, and we should be careful not to assume that a question is a statement of His judgement and condemnation. Jesus asked over

300 hundred questions in the bible. Questions from God are more like invitations to explore and expand in a relationship than to end conversation and pronounce the victor.

The first question is *"why are you angry?"*. Anger is a response to a process that we have encountered inwardly or outwardly. It is an indication of something that has happened. Anger is not bad, but what you do with it can be very bad. The confrontation of anger is one point of maturing that must be trained and curbed into the proper place. What is done with our anger will often be the prophetic indication of how our future will play out. Ephesians 4:26 "Be ye angry, and sin not: let not the sun go down upon your wrath" (KJV). The reality of anger is there to alert us that something has gone wrong in our systems. It is like an internal alarm system that is established and then helps us to respond to the thing that has triggered the alarm. There is value to our anger. Don't let the valuable alarm push you to destroy the thing that the alarm is there to serve. The caution of not allowing the sun to go down on your anger is saying that when there is an alarm (anger) don't allow it to go into darkness and be hidden. The sun is an illuminator in our lives and when it goes down, we lose light to see. When we get angry, we should face it to see what the alarm is saying while there is light to see and respond to the alarm appropriately. If we allow our anger to flourish and fester in the dark, we put ourselves in a position to be poisoned, unaware of the dissemination of its influence. Anger is a powerful thing, and we should face it in the light with the people who love us. So here we have God asking Cain, "Why are you angry?". He is not telling him not to be angry. God is asking why he is angry. In the pursuit of the why is growth and development into maturity.

The second question is, "*Why has your countenance fallen?*". The word for countenance is, you guessed it, face or "*paniym*" in Hebrew. Why does God ask Cain about his face in the midst of his offering not being regarded? Another aspect of the maturing process is revealed. Not only is understanding anger important, but how we hold our face when something goes contrary to our expectation is important. Some may phrase it as what do you look at, or to, when things go wrong. The positioning of our face in the midst of adversity is one of the most important things we can learn and the greatest indications of our maturity. What does the child do at night when he is afraid of something? Does he not hide his face? What Cain did with his face shows how he responded to disappointment, failure, shame, embarrassment, jealousy, rejection, sadness, anger, or however he processed the interaction. The mature know how to face the truth and the reality of whatever situation they are in. Cain allowed his face to fall. To have a fallen face positions us to look at the ground. It doesn't give us a positive outlook. Having a fallen face lessens our vision. Looking downward decreases our awareness and alertness of our environment and others around us. To allow our face to fall communicates to ourselves and others that we have not conducted ourselves in a worthy manner. The fallen countenance communicates physiologically. I think the most damaging thing about allowing our face to fall is that we cut ourselves off from the face-to-face relationships that we need in that time. In the midst of anger and whatever situation we face, maturity is to be humble and keep our countenance on the Lord.

After the two questions the Lord asks He says, "If thou doest well, shalt thou not be accepted? And if thou doest not well, sin lieth at the door. And unto thee shall be his desire, and thou shalt rule over him" (KJV). When something isn't well due to our action, we face the point of sin. The Lord never told Cain that he had sinned in his offering. Cain had fallen short of something, then sin was at his door when he was angry and looking down. This is an important distinction. Cain's offering was different than Abel's and God did not look to Cain's, but that doesn't mean that his offering was sinful. Cain had not done wrong; he just hadn't done well. It was not the best or maybe what God was looking for, and sin came to desire him at the point of his anger and fallen countance. So, in not doing well, sin came and desired Cain. Cain could have ruled over sin and should have learned how to do that. To learn how to rule over sin is a work of discipline. Jesus Christ ruled over sin. He learned this by having a relationship with the Father. Jesus was angry and did not sin, and He kept His countenance upon the Father. Cain's anger and his fallen countenance played out in his choice to kill his brother and be punished by the Lord. The punishment was too great in Cain's perspective, and he reveals the severity of it by saying that he will be driven from the face of the ground and hidden from the Lord's face. Cain realized the importance of the face of the ground and the Lord's face and based his appeal on that. In Cain's appeal, there is an intimation that he knew of the curse on the ground that was told to his father Adam. The face of the earth had been cursed to be hard and produce lack through toil. Thorns and thistles and sorrow were the fruit of the earth's face. So, in the process of maturing, we can see that our face plays a vital role. The training of discipline reveals how to deal with anger and how to hold our face. The direction of our face will often be the direction of our steps.

Another great story of the face in the maturing process is that of Jacob. Let's look at Genesis 32:22-32. This is the story of Jacob wrestling and prevailing with God and men. In this process, Jacob's name is changed to Israel, which means "he who strives with God". Jacob is wrestling with a man before daybreak, and he is holding his own in the struggle. The man touched the socket of his hip and caused Jacob to have a limp, but Jacob would not relent until he received a blessing. Jacob then reveals what has happened at the end of the story saying, "I have seen God face to face, yet my life has been preserved" (NASB). Jacob named the place that he wrestled Peniel, which means "the face of God" or "facing God". In the maturing process, we have times that we wrestle in the dark before dawn has broken upon us. These are times of darkness not in a bad sense but in a sense of mystery and the unknown. The wrestling with God and man is part of the maturing process. It is interesting that his name is changed through the interaction of seeing God face to face and living. Our names are carriers of our identity and destiny. For Jacob to say that he saw God face to face is a claim of mystery because the text reads that he wrestled with a man and that it was in a context of not much light. Seeing the face of God doesn't always happen in the light and glory of the noonday sun. We often grow and mature more in the night when our vision is less clear but our determination in those times is more transformative.

This story illustrates that to see the face of God or to face him doesn't mean that all will be easy or that we will escape without a limp. We do receive a blessing, and our name is changed revealing more of who we are. There are going to be times in the maturing process that you find yourself alone at night having to wrestle with God and man. You will find that these times are ones in which you will see the face of God and be changed. The hip alignment of your life will be set anew enabling you to walk in the fullness of the new name that he gives you. Wrestling is an important skill in life. It is training in a very intimate way. Grappling can lead to respect, appreciation, honor, and love.

Love, what else is there if there isn't love? When it comes to maturity love may not be the thing that comes to mind but it should. Remember that love is the reason behind discipline. Discipline without love is just a desire to control or manipulate. Love is not just the reason for discipline but also a driving force in the midst of it. In the love chapter of 1 Corinthians 13 we find a reality of maturity that once again points to the face as having an important role. Paul writes in verse 9-12:

> "For we know in part, and we prophesy in part. But when that which is perfect is come, then that which is in part shall be done away. When I was a child, I spake as a child, I understood as a child, I thought as a child: but when I became a man, I put away childish things. For now we see through a glass, darkly; but then face to face: now I know in part; but then shall I know even as also I am known" (KJV).

Paul writes comparatively to reveal what is and also

what shall be. This first comparison is the partiality of what we know and prophesy to the perfect that comes and makes the partial done away with. The second comparison is that of the child's speaking, thinking, and reasoning to having become a man and done away with childish things. The third comparison is between seeing through a glass darkly and seeing face to face. The fourth comparison is knowing in part versus knowing fully on the basis of being fully known. These comparisons all have obvious progressions that show maturity and the areas that maturity plays out. Those areas are knowledge, prophecy, speaking, thinking, reasoning, and seeing. In the progression of maturity from incomplete to the complete Paul identifies going from a variety of things to the greatest and complete, which is love. Love is the ultimate. Love is the reason and the purpose and the fullness to live in.

The main point for us in this writing of Paul is the key he gives in verse 12. The comparison of how we see. We can see in a glass darkly or face to face. When we lack love, we are immature and only see through a glass darkly. When we are mature, we walk in love and have face-to-face relationships. The face-to-face relationship is the fullness of love in how we see. The fullness of love is seen in the face-to-face relationship. This is the third example of how important our face is. This truth that Paul is sharing ties perfectly with the one of the proverbs of Solomon. You probably have heard the phrase "iron sharpens iron." This comes from the book of Proverbs chapter 27 verse 17. It is a great phrase and applicable in life, but it is not the whole verse. The second part of the verse says, "so a man sharpeneth the countenance of his friend" (KJV). Most of us connect the reality of iron sharpening iron with the idea that we are made better, and we grow when we come into contact with challenging people or circumstances. While it is true that other people and circumstances can improve our sharpness and strength, we are missing the fullness of what God has designed if we don't realize that the transformation of our face comes from the interaction and engagement of our friend's face. Iron sharpening iron is not the picture where we are to stop. That picture is to help us see the value of the face of our friend. We may not always like what happens in the dynamic of having to see our friend's face. It may produce sparks and pain, but the sharpening of our face into our true identity comes through the face of our friend. Jesus said, "greater love has no one than this, that a person will lay down his life for his friends" (NASB). Why did Jesus include that reality of friends? He could have just said greater love has no one than a person laying down his life. I believe that he included the reality of the friend because this is truly love. Love lives and dies without a mask, face to face. Jesus Christ, God made flesh, is love, and he chose to come face to face with us. One of the downfalls of a mask is that they require quickness. For a mask to be effective it can't be looked at for too long. Friendship lives in longevity and seeing each other not in glances of life but in consistent, sustained, and intense periods. If you see someone in a mask and look long enough the mask is never sufficient to sustain the identity. Look at the mask long enough and you will start to see through it. Look at a friend long enough and you will start to be challenged and transformed by it. Jesus, the incarnation of love, came to look and see us in the face. If we choose to look him in the face we will grow, mature and be transformed. To grow up and mature is synonymous with face-to-face relationships. Face to face relationship is the reality of love.

Maturing in life is not about killing parts of ourselves that God has designed and created. Suicide is not God's way of maturing. We have to recognize that to kill our emotions, mind, will, heart, creativity, passion, desire, relationships or body is going to result in death not life. It is not about killing a part of yourself so that you don't have to face the pain, shame, guilt or whatever may be there. God desires that you have life and life abundantly. C.S. Lewis said,

> "When I became a man, I put away childish things, including the fear of childishness and the desire to be very grown up."

Your goal should not be the image you create for yourself. It isn't profitable to gain the whole world and lose your soul, but discipline is good for us so that we may share in His holiness. Maturity is having genuine relationships that allow for the flourishing of who you are and those around you. Genuine relationship face-to-face is where our capability, character, responsibility, and accountability find their fullness, and we love one another as God has loved us. In a face-to-face relationship with God, ourselves, and others we can receive discipline and grow into the full stature of who we are to be.

CHAPTER 4
THE HEAVENLY
FACE LIFT

If you don't like your face don't worry; it can be changed. In our age we are obsessed with selfies and the changing of our face through surgery, fillers, filters, or cosmetics. I wonder sometimes if all of that is the fruit of failed relationships. I am not here to say that it is all vanity and chasing after the wind. Maybe there is something intuitive in it. Maybe there is a deep awareness in all of us that our faces aren't living up to some standard. Maybe, in all the things we do to our face, there is something noble that we are trying to pursue – something better – something more.

How do we get the more? How do we get a better face? God's ways are great, and he has given us a way to get a heavenly facelift.

There was a line to a song I heard when I was a kid that my mom would sing in the house. It came from a concert by Kim Clement, and he sang, "Somewhere in the future you look a lot better than you do right now." I remember that she used to sing this at home sometimes to my brother and me. I appreciated her hope, encouragement, and vision of better things for us. I didn't know if I always looked better in the future than I did then, but the important thing was the message. We all need hope. We all need vision. In the United States, I believe we carry this message of hope. Whether you believe in the American dream or think this is a land of opportunity, you need hope. We need some message of change. We might look bad right now, but it isn't going to be like this forever. If we lose our hope, we lose our vision and become nihilistic. The man that has no hope, will soon not have a face at all.

We all go through things that will mess up our face, leaving us scarred, maimed, and in shock having to face life on the defensive. This wasn't God's original intent. Stuff happens – deception, rebellion, isolation, separation were all major factors in the original plan getting offtrack. We aren't going to discuss why and how all that played out in the early generations of humanity. Hopefully, we can agree that our faces aren't perfect. Our focus is on what God and we can do about the imperfection so that we no longer live on the defensive.

In the scriptures. we find the story of the sons of Korah. Korah and about 250 men had rebelled against Moses being the leader that God had established, and in their rebellion, were challenged to stand before the Lord to see if Moses' words would be honored by the Lord. Moses' words and position were honored by God and the earth opened and swallowed the men and their possessions alive (Numbers 16). Some descendants of Korah that survived would go on to pen some of the great Psalms we have today. The descendants that survived were not part of the rebellion but were probably aware of the story and affected by the serious consequences of Korah's action. Psalm 42 was one of the psalms they wrote. In this psalm we find the heavenly face lift.

"As the hart panteth after the water brooks, so panteth my soul after thee, O God. My soul thirsteth for God, for the living God: when shall I come and appear before God? My tears have been my meat day and night, while they continually say unto me, Where is thy God? When I remember these things, I pour out my soul in me: for I had gone with the multitude, I went with them to the house of God, with the voice of joy and praise, with a multitude that kept holyday. Why art thou cast down, O my soul? and why art thou disquieted in me? hope thou in God: for I shall yet praise him for the help of his countenance. O my God, my soul is cast down within me: therefore will I remember thee from the land of Jordan, and of the Hermonites, from the hill Mizar. Deep calleth unto deep at the noise of thy waterspouts: all thy waves and thy billows are gone over me. Yet the Lord will command his lovingkindness in the day time, and in the night his song shall be with me, and my prayer unto the God of my life. I will say unto God my rock, Why hast thou forgotten me? why go I mourning because of the oppression of the enemy? As with a sword in my bones, mine enemies reproach me; while they say daily unto me, Where is thy God? Why art thou cast down, O my soul? and why art thou disquieted within me? hope thou in God: for I shall yet praise him, who is the health of my countenance, and my God" Psalm 42 (KJV).

You may recognize this psalm for its poetic beauty and the vivid imagery, but I believe that a key to the despair of our soul is identified. In verse one through four the author reveals the state of his soul. His soul is *"longing for the water brooks, thirsting for God, waiting to see God, crying, remembering the good times,* and *being poured out within him"*. This is a desperate state: a state of despair and exhaustion. Then, in verse five, he begins to speak directly to his soul and ask why it is cast down and disturbed within him. Something has caused his soul to be in this state. This questioning is the first part of the face-lift. We must identify our face and the condition it is in. In verse one, he has looked at himself and his own face. This is him looking at the reality of his identity and soul. It could be that he does not recognize that looking at the condition of his soul is looking at himself face to face, but that is exactly what is happening.

The next part of the process is that he begins to command his soul to hope in God. This is telling his soul to wait on God and to make his hope God. To hope in God is to put himself in the position of God's responsibility. Hope contains expectancy. A good image of this is when we go to the doctor, we are putting ourselves in the position of expectation that the doctor is going to be able to respond to us. So, we go to the doctor's office and sit in his waiting room and then wait in the exam or operating room for him to respond to our situation according to his expertise. This picture of how hope works shows us that hope has a lot to do with position. It is a position of our physical body but also our soul body in the expectation that the doctor can respond to us. So, he tells his soul to hope in God and then says that he will yet praise him. This praise is a recognition that when he is positioned in the expectation of God's care, he will come out of that position with praise to God. He knows that something is going to change and that the change that God works is worthy of praise. I know that our earthly experience with doctors doesn't always result in the betterment of our health, but when it does, we celebrate a doctor's clean bill of health. All the hoping in God and the change that will be worthy of praise is because of the last phrase of verse five, *"for the help of his countenance."* God's countenance, His face, is the reason. God's face, when revealed to us, is the basis of our relationship and transformation. The word for help means salvation. The help of God's face is salvation for us and our soul. To see Him face to face is going to be salvation for us. Seeing Him face to face means that we will see his glory, his character, his identity, his substance, love, life, light, grace, and peace. We will see true meaning, purpose, destiny, and the salvation we need.

Then the psalm continues with what would be somewhat of a repetition telling of what is happening with his life. The despair of the soul is still there, but there is more of a direct communication with God now. There is remembrance of God from important places of previous encounters with God. There is an explanation to some degree of what has happened with the deep and God's waves and billows. Speaking to his soul once more, he is declaring what God will do recognized as a prayer. As the author engages his soul there are questions that he is going to ask God, and that is an important allowance that we have in our relationship with God. But in the closing verse there is a return to the same reality of verse five. He asks his soul "why" and gives the admonition to his soul to once more hope in God and that he will yet praise him. The last part of the verse is slightly different though. The last part of the verse includes, "*the health of my countenance and my God*". The difference is that it has changed from the help of His face to the health, which is the same Hebrew word as help, of my face. It is the same phrase recognized in its fullness. The reason for praise is the same said slightly different. First, the reason to praise is because of the help of His face. The second reason to praise is because the help of my face and my God. Here is the progression played out and recognized in the author. He has seen how the heavenly face lift transforms and plays out. Recall the doctor's office example. We are glad when the doctor shows up or comes in to meet with us. There is an initial recognition of the help that we know his face and presence brings. Then, once he has given his advice, we realize that his direction, input, or changes are altering our face.

Remember that he asks in verse two when shall he come and appear before God. This is an expectation to see God face-to-face. This is the beginning of the heavenly face-lift. The process of Psalm forty-two is one where the despair and problem is identified, and the soul is told to hope in God. The reason for hoping in God is that this puts you in the position of expecting that God is going to respond. When we recognize that God will reveal himself to us and we will see the salvation of His face, there will be things that come up, but it will culminate with the help of His face being the help of our face. Our face is lifted when we appear before God, honest with our soul and see the help of His face. To see the help of His face is to see the help of our face and be transformed.

Paul understood this process. He experienced it in

his salvation transformation on the road to Damascus when the Lord was revealed to him, and he was changed forever. He would then write to the Corinthian church in his second letter to them saying in chapter 3:18, "But we all, with open face beholding as in a glass the glory of the Lord, are changed into the same image from glory to glory, even as by the Spirit of the Lord" (KJV). The open face is one where the veil, or maybe we could even say mask, is removed. Beholding the glory of the Lord, we are changed. This change isn't a slight adjustment. In the Greek, the word is metamorphoō, which is, "to transform, transfigure, to experience metamorphose". This is the process of the larva to the butterfly. While Paul identifies this transforming process, he also identifies where the transformation comes from. The last part of the verse shows that this happens by the Spirit of the Lord. When we are face-to-face with the Lord, the Spirit transforms us from glory to glory. It is a continuation of glory to more glory.

This is the heavenly face lift that we all could use. This is how we receive the more, the better, the fullness of what God intends for our identity. It's great that we don't have to do our own face surgery. We don't have to depend on ourselves to transform ourselves: look to God; appear before God; stand face to face with Him unveiled; be honest with your soul; know and trust that the Spirit of the Lord will transform you. For you will praise Him yet again as you see the glory that He will establish in you, the same image of Him. This is what the intent of God is for you. He wants you to look like Him. There is hope. God has made a way for you to experience a heavenly facelift.

CHAPTER 5

THE FOUR

FACES OF GOD

D oes God literally have four faces? He may. We know that he has a face, but to explain or describe his face is too hard for any one man. We know that as man we need help. It is hard enough to figure out ourselves and our own face. Thankfully, God didn't leave us to our own devices and understanding. To think of God's face is beyond our human capacity. Our capacity is so limited in the grasping of God, yet He doesn't abandon us. God is so gracious and merciful in understanding our weakness, blindness, deafness, and our willful ignorance. The miracle of the incarnation is so much more than God becoming flesh and dwelling among us. The incarnation is God emptying Himself so that He might be counted among us and that we might be counted among Him. This seems to be the most inclusive thing that anyone has done for us as humans. He includes Himself in us so that we may be included in Him. The beauty of the incarnation is that it was a revelation of God's plan and His inclusion of us into His way and His life. The glory of the incarnation is the beginning of oneness.

The incarnation of God in the person of Jesus Christ, the Word who became flesh and dwelt among us full of grace and truth, the glory of the only begotten from the Father, this is God's story. It is His story being revealed to us through the Virgin Mary in the town of Bethlehem, in the humble abode of the manger. I often marvel at the reality that God, the inexpressible, infinite, unfathomable, omniscient, omnipotent, eternal, unsearchable, Creator of all things has made Himself communicable. The writer of Hebrews says that His son is the radiance of His glory and the exact representation of His nature. This son is Jesus Christ. Jesus' story is found in the four gospels of Matthew, Mark, Luke, and John. In these four accounts of Jesus' life, we can see His face and know the face of God as His spirit reveals Himself to us. Just because you read someone's story doesn't necessarily mean that you have seen that person. The written account of the gospels isn't everything, but it is a great start in seeing the face of God. The gospels don't claim to tell everything about Jesus, and they don't claim to be the finality of what God is revealing about Himself. Each gospel is written for a purpose and in each one we see the plan of God in His infinite wisdom.

In the end of John's gospel, he writes, "And there are also many other things which Jesus did, the which, if they should be written everyone, I suppose that even the world itself could not contain the books that should be written. Amen" (John 21:25 KJV). All that Jesus did is not what John, or the other disciples were trying to record. The question to be asked when we read the gospel accounts should be more purposeful and specific rather than generic. We should ask what God is revealing in this account and why. The gospel is the good news of God. So, we ask what good news is being revealed in this face of Jesus' story. This doesn't mean there are four different gospels. It does mean and show that the story of God's face being revealed cannot be told by one man. There is one reality of good news, and it is the same in each account. That good news is God revealing Himself in the face of Jesus of Nazareth, the Christ our Lord. There is one Jesus Christ, and He is the one that the gospels declare.

Imagine if the story of your life had to be written out for all of humanity to read. Who would you choose to write your story? There are many people in your life whose input would be required to accomplish this task. Quickly you find there isn't just one person who could write your story. There isn't one person who knows it all, and the people who may know a lot of it would still be limited to their perspective. Your mom and dad could tell the story of your birth and childhood, but they would tell it according to their perspective. What mom sees as important is probably very different from what dad sees as important. It wouldn't mean that one of them was right or wrong in their story of you. They could both be right at the same time. Take some time and write out what you would want your story to be and who you would want to tell it. What do you think they would say and what would you want them to say? What will your story reveal? What is the purpose of your story? What makes your story unique? This thought experiment is what happens at your funeral and the time spent in the grieving process. Hopefully, it isn't your parents telling the story, but your spouse, kids, coworkers, friends, and people that you have impacted. No one demands that only one person can tell the story of your life. That would be an unreasonable expectation. Our lives are complicated and filled with complexities beyond the scope of one person's account. The wise path for our story is for it to be told by more than one person.

God has chosen the wise path of more than one person writing His story and still acknowledging that it isn't all of it. If our stories couldn't be told by one person, then God's story isn't going to be seen in one account of His story. Who has God chosen to tell His story? Ultimately, He wants all of us to tell His story, but in the written account of the scriptures the accounts of Matthew, Mark, Luke, and John have been chosen. These gospels weren't chosen by men and assembled at some counsel of man. These are the ones that ultimately revealed themselves as being the true gospels of Jesus Christ. A great book to read on this question is *Who Chose the Gospels* by C.E. Hill.

Why did God choose four gospels? There were other options and there were other disciples that could have written an account of Jesus' life. I believe that the number four carries a significance that fits with the pattern of God's story. Four is often tied to creation and material completeness. The fourth letter of the Hebrew alphabet is *dalet* which is a door. It would be fitting that the one who said "I am the door" would have four accounts of His story. The river that flowed out of Eden to water the garden that God made divided into four rivers in Genesis 2:10-14. We have four elements, four cardinal directions, four seasons, and four major lunar phases. The number four speaks to creation and manifesting things in creation. In the scriptures, there are ample occurrences of the number four. E.W.

Bullinger has compiled some great information on the number four in his book *Number in Scripture*. Some of the examples he gives of the number four are the four soils in Matthew, four kinds of flesh in 1 Corinthians, four people whose name was changed, four kings in Daniel, four things little and wise in Proverbs, four times rainbow is mentioned in scripture, four times the Hebrew word for the branch is mentioned, and the four times the Greek word for lamb is mentioned.

One specific use of the number four is in the revelation of the cherubim in Ezekiel and the living creatures in Revelation. In Ezekiel chapter one Ezekiel saw a vision of God and when he described it, there were four living beings that each had four faces. The form of their faces was of a man, lion, bull, and eagle. Above the four living beings was a structure of a throne and one on the throne that had the appearance of a man. This is a glorious vision. Then, in chapter ten, they are called cherubim and Ezekiel engages with them and the coals that were in their whirling wheels. He then describes them again saying that each one had four faces. The first face was the face of the cherub, then the face of a man, the face of the lion and the face of the eagle. These four cherubim each had four faces. Then we find John writing of the heavenly scene in chapter four of Revelation where he describes four living creatures in the center and around the throne. The four living creatures in Revelation are not described as having four faces each, but each one is like the creature. The first is like a lion, the second like a calf, the third had a face like that of a man, and the fourth like a flying eagle. There are some differences between these listings, but the four descriptions are there for a reason. They are all tied to the throne of God and the release of His Word, glory, and presence.

Does God have four faces? Not according to a material understanding, but when you look at God's throne, presence, glory, and the structures that are around Him, you must acknowledge that the faces closest to His and what we would see, are the four faces of the cherubim or living creatures. These heavenly beings have been expounded upon since they were first mentioned in the book of Genesis guarding the way to the Tree of Life with a flaming sword (Genesis 3:24). God expresses and reveals Himself in the creation that He creates. The ones first around His throne are these four faces. Literally, I think we would have to say that the face of God is the face of Jesus Christ whatever He would have looked like when He walked the earth as the incarnation of the Word. To say that God's face is that of Jesus is correct, yet lacking in a way because we don't know that much about Jesus's physical life. Also, Paul tells us in 1 Corinthians 5:16, "Wherefore henceforth know we no man after the flesh: yea, though we have known Christ after the flesh, yet now henceforth know we him no more". In addition to, when He was raised from the dead, His disciples had some confusion about His appearance as well as when John described Him in Revelation one, His face was like the sun shining in its strength. Also, the prophecy in Isaiah 52:14 of God's servant says, "As many were astonied at thee; his visage was so marred more than any man, and his form more than the sons of men:..." With all of these dynamics about the literal form of Jesus' flesh, one might be hard pressed to only grasp at a physical form of a face of God. I am not negating the reality that Jesus has a literal face but would caution anyone to set in concrete their idea of

Jesus' physical face.

It could be said that God has four faces, not in a literal sense of flesh, but in the literal sense that He reveals Himself in the four faces of the gospels. He has given us as the good news by the incarnation of Jesus Christ in the face of the four gospels, which are seen as the four faces that are expressed around His throne. The history of Christianity has proved this out with the recognition of the gospels representing these four faces. Some of the earliest writings we have of Christians show that they too saw this connection and saw it as a way of God. Irenaeus, Victorinus, Jerome and Augustine made this connection of the faces to the gospels and most likely they were not the ones who came up with the idea, but the ones whose writings we have record of. They don't all agree on which face corresponds to each gospel for they see a different working of God and make their own connections of meaning. God has revealed His face in the person of Jesus Christ and the scriptures of the four gospels tell a large part of that revealing.

I will show that the parallel of the four gospels to the four faces is as follows. The gospel of Matthew is the face of the lion. The gospel of Mark is the face of the ox/cherub/calf. The gospel of Luke is the face of the man. The gospel of John is the face of the flying eagle. The reason that I see this order is the subject of the rest of the book. Whether you totally agree or see a differentiation with my list, remember that the purpose is to see God's face and His revealing in your life.

The gospels are biography and story. The Word incarnates in the flesh. Jesus incarnated in the story of the gospels. The gospel is incarnated in our lives by the Holy Spirit.

CHAPTER 6

INTRODUCTION TO THE LAYOUT OF THE FOUR FACES

This chapter is going to provide the outline for the next four chapters each covering one of the faces and the corresponding gospel. The chapters for the four faces are written in a study outline format that address each gospels uniqueness and the differentiations that reveal how they express the face of God. So, this chapter provides an understanding of what each category is, means, and how it is applied in our lives.

Thus far we have covered God's Face, Your Face, Maturity, The Heavenly Face Lift, and the Four Faces of God. These chapters provide a framework of understanding so that we can engage the four gospels in a transformative way. The transformative work takes place as you engage God's face and your own face through the four Gospels. This material on the four gospels is not a comparative analysis for informational proofs. The material is not a historical defense for their credibility. Hopefully, at this point in the book you have concluded that the gospels have immense value and that they are genuine accounts of the story of God's incarnation in the person of Jesus Christ. This study is not a total accounting of each gospel's unique telling. I pray that the Holy Spirit will guide you into more understanding and a greater relationship with God, through the door of Jesus Christ. The information outlined of each gospel is so that we can see and grow in our love for God and what he has done for us in revealing Himself to us. This material will help you to grow in your knowledge and understanding of each gospel, but this is only to the purpose that you may grow in your relationship with God. From your growth and the maturing of your relationship with God, you will begin to see that your face is changed. When your face is transformed, and you understand what you look like as he conforms you into the image of the son, then you will be better equipped to shine as the light of God that you are. Remember the desire of Jesus was so that we could be one with Him. In the least, oneness means that the story of the gospel is also a story of us.

Let's begin looking at the outline for the face in each gospel. Each outline will begin with a **general description** of the gospel that identifies the key themes of the gospel. The theme of the gospel is important to the details that each author will bring forth in that gospel. These themes will be revealed in the whole of the gospel.

Next is the **key** of each gospel. The key of the gospel isn't what unlocks the gospel, but it is what that face needs to operate in, for the fullness of the purpose of God to come forth. Any scripture is only revealed by God's Spirit and having relationship with him. The key of the gospel is that we will see and understand more of God and will bring forth more of our identity that God has destined us for. This shows not only what Jesus fulfills in the gospel but also how we, being like him will have this focus in our life. This is an important application point for us as we grow, and our face becomes like His. As we grow and God develops that face in us the key is what we are to focus on. The key is the purpose of why God is developing that face in you. When you see the key of the gospel you start to see more fully the beauty of God and his story manifested for a specific reason.

With each key, a lock of some kind is implied. Each gospel has what I call a **challenge** or issue that must be faced. The challenge is the lock that will try to prevent the face from coming forth and accomplishing God's purpose. Jesus had to face challenges and He had to learn how to overcome those challenges without succumbing to a lesser identity in dealing with them. As we grow in that face of God, we will also have to face challenges. We know that just because we are Christians it does not mean that all the challenges or hardships are dealt with. We must face those challenges and learn as Jesus did. Every challenge will present an opportunity for us to choose what image we will be. Paul, in Romans 1:22-23 writes, "Professing themselves to be wise, they became fools, And changed the glory of the uncorruptible God into an image made like to corruptible man, and to birds, and four-footed beasts, and creeping things" (KJV). This is an example of what happens when we decide that we know best for ourselves. We are created in the image of God, and He desires that we walk in His uncorruptible glory. We were and are intended for the glory of God. When a challenge comes we always have a choice of how to respond. Jesus had to choose and so do we. There is no escaping the choice during a challenge.

Did you catch that Paul listed four things that the glory of God was exchanged for? These four images parallel the four faces and are the lesser image of glory for each one of them. They are applied in the order that they are written. So, in the challenge of each gospel we will also look at **the lesser image of glory** that we don't want to take on as our face.

Confrontation is a reality of life. You are going to be confronted by people and things. It goes with the whole idea of challenge. Jesus faced challenges and was confronted. The people that confronted Jesus didn't have a goal in mind of helping him to truly be who he was supposed to be; however, we have help. As we mature, we need to be confronted by the Lord and those around us that God has put in our life to help us be who we are to be. This confrontation section has to do with how we can confront each other in a way that will help to face the challenges and choose the face that God is bringing forth. Also in leadership, which we will talk about in a later chapter, we will see that confronting those in leadership can be done in a way that helps them to focus on their purpose and walk in the glory that God is releasing through them. Confrontation is a way of helping those in our lives in the development of their face. If someone is getting off course, there is a way to call them to remember who they are to be and act accordingly. Confrontation isn't about condemning or proving someone wrong. The purpose of our confrontations should be to call each person to their true identity and help them to live in the reality of what God has called them to.

Genealogy is a big deal. The Jewish people and the prophecies of their Messiah were tied to a genealogy that was specific. So, we will look at how each face presents the genealogy of Jesus. The genealogies of our life reveal key items and trends for our lives. Genealogies are like roots through history budding forth stolons of new lives.

Next isn't a specific thing, but a collection of points that reveal the face of the gospel. I call these **notes**. The notes for each gospel include unique things that show the reality of that face. Some of these notes are comparative to other gospels and some are unique to that gospel alone. These illustrate the face of God in the gospel. The notes are organized and written to show the revealing of the themes of that face.

The next section will be **Judas**. My brother brought to me one day the reality of Judas and that Jesus never got rid of the betrayer. That has stuck with me. Yes, Judas served a purpose in the plan of God. That is easy to say, but when you realize that Jesus chose Judas to be one of his twelve disciples and included him in some of the most intimate relations of the disciples, we realize there is something more to it. The betrayer could have been a disciple that wasn't one of the twelve. Jesus could have shielded himself from what He knew was in Judas, but He didn't. We all have to face betrayal and it often comes from those that we have chosen to be in our lives. Each gospel shows how to deal with betrayal and the betrayer. We will look at how Jesus did this so that we too can respond from that reality of his face and not our own ways. The question we ask is, how should we, having the faces of God, respond to betrayal. That's a big one.

Redemption: don't we all love a good redemption

story. Jesus is our redeemer. We couldn't talk about Jesus' story and not see redemption. This section targets redemption from a different angle. Jesus redeems us by His blood, the cross, His sacrifice, His resurrection, His life, and His love, but we are going to focus on the **redemptive woman.** There are four women in the genealogy of Jesus before Mary, His mother, and they show how God redeems through the four faces of each gospel. Women play a major role in Jesus' life and ministry, yet He doesn't downplay their importance. The feminine principle is necessary in creation. The masculine can have a seed, but the seed needs a womb in which to grow and develop. We will look at how each face has a redemptive feminine principle that helps us to experience redemption in our lives. Now, Jesus isn't redeemed by these women. He didn't need redeeming. The redemptive woman shows how each face can be redeemed when we make a choice contrary to having the glorious face that God intends for us. Remember the four images Paul mentioned that are a lesser glory? Jesus didn't take on these lesser images, but we have. Thus, God reveals redemption through the redemptive women. In Genesis, the promised seed that crushes the head of the serpent comes through the woman. The woman, the feminine principal, births the seed of redemption. Mary is the woman who gave birth to Jesus and stayed with Him throughout His whole story, even being at the cross. We aren't going to cover Mary in the four redemptive women but will stay focused on how the four women in His genealogy show redemption for the four faces.

Lastly, we will cover the **end of the gospel**. We will look at how each gospel concludes and what that reveals about the face of that gospel. This will include looking at the commission that Jesus gives. Usually, the commission is identified with one gospel, but each gospel has a commission. The end of the gospel doesn't mean that the story is over because the story is going to continue. Each face has a release into what God continues to do. The face of each gospel doesn't end with Jesus, and His commissioning ties back into the key of each face. The end shows how God redeems and fulfills the purpose of God setting up its continuation. So, the end of the gospel section covers how each face's purpose will continue to shine forth and go forth in and as us. We are disciples. We are the learners of Jesus. We are those who become like Him in His image, in His light, in His life, in His glory, and in His love.

One encouragement that I would challenge you is to read the scriptures for yourself. Study them. We won't have enough space to include all the scriptures so take the time to read them in their full context. Remember that the purpose of this information is not to just build your database of information. This is for you to engage the face of God and be transformed as you walk out your relationship with God.

Applying this information in your life occurs by intention. Here are some steps that will help you to engage each face and the different aspects. Read and engage the scriptures with the awareness that they are written for you so that you can grow. Pray the faces and aspects of each face, acknowledging God in each one. An example would be:

"Lord, I thank you that you revealed yourself as the ox, the one who is the sacrificial servant laying down your life. You are the one who strengthens and empowers me in true service to those that you have brought into my life. I am a witness to the reality of your redemption as I lay down my life and as I plow the fields that you have called me to. Thank you for the times of prayer in which you lead and guide so that I am not led by man or the voice of others but by the relationship that I have with you. Lord, I let go of false images and lesser forms of glory so that you may be glorified in my life by the release of the glory that you designed me for. Lord in the midst of betrayal let me stay focused on what you are calling me to so that I may continue to serve you. Thank you for commissioning me and the awareness that there is work to be done for your kingdom and glory..."

Also, begin to pay attention to the leaders in your life, so that you will start to see the characteristics of each face in them. Begin to ask which face you resonate with and start to honor those characteristics of God, in you.

CHAPTER 7

THE LION

The first face of God is the Lion. The gospel of Matthew is the face of the Lion. The gospel of Matthew was written by Matthew, the tax collector mentioned in chapter 10 as one of the twelve apostles. The face of Matthew the Lion reveals the themes of kingdom, territory, dominion, kingship, royalty, righteousness, and mountains. This is the face of the lion of the tribe of Judah. From the prophecy of Jacob to his sons in Genesis 49, where Judah is a lion's whelp, to the book of Revelation chapter five where John is told to "stop weeping; behold the lion of the tribe of Judah, the root of David, has overcome so as to open the book and its seven seals," (NASB), the lion is fulfilled in the person of Jesus. The lion is concerned with those who are to be a part of his kingdom. A lion is aware of his territory and dominion. The king is over his kingdom, and it is serious business. The way that Matthew the Lion shows forth the true kingdom and overcomes the other kingdoms is by revealing the reality of Jesus' righteousness, the fulfillment of prophecies and that he is worthy of worship.

The Key

"And she shall bring forth a son, and thou shalt call his name Jesus: for he shall save his people from their sins." "Behold, a virgin shall be with child, and shall bring forth a son, and they shall call his name Emmanuel, which being interpreted is, God with us" (1:21,23 KJV). The key is to save his people from their sins by being God with us. The lion can fight and has tremendous power, but the purpose is not focused on other kings. The focus is to recognize the people to save from their sins. The power, royalty, and kingship are used not for self but to bring and establish salvation for the people from their sins. Salvation for his people – to bring them into His kingdom – is the focus from which there shall be no distraction.

The Challenge

Salvation is not an easy task to accomplish. When the king of all kings comes to save His people, He must face other kings and kingdoms. The challenge for the lion is to not attack earthly kingdoms even though they try to kill him. The fighting that Jesus does is always from His position and kingdom. In chapter 2:1-3 it says,

> "Now when Jesus was born in Bethlehem of Judaea in the days of Herod the king, behold, there came wise men from the east to Jerusalem, Saying, Where is he that is born King of the Jews? for we have seen his star in the east, and are come to worship him. When Herod the king had heard these things, he was troubled, and all Jerusalem with him" (KJV).

Notice that Jesus' birth is marked by the earthly kingdom of Herod. Jesus is called "the King of the

Jews." When the face of the lion was born, Herod and all of Jerusalem was troubled. The troubling of the earthly kingdoms is a part of the ministry of the lion. When a lion shows up, the lesser kings and kingdoms feel threatened by the presence of the lion. As you grow in your identity carrying that lion face, you will have to be careful not to fight the earthly kingdoms in earthly ways.

Lesser image of glory

The glory of God that the lion exchanges is the image of corruptible man. Corruptible man is the idea of the perfect man in a worldly sense. This perfect man is one that fights for himself and his kingdom by directly fighting the kingdoms of man. This battle of kings and kingdoms is also why the lion doesn't exchange for the lesser image of the four-footed beast. The lion is about kingship and the corruptible man is the fallen image that will try to be the ultimate king. This man defends himself over others. It is the man that will do whatever it takes to prove himself perfect. Arguing even in the midst of obvious wrong that the fault isn't theirs, they will prove themselves to be righteous by any means. The perfect man is the classic image of that guy or girl that is better than everyone else and doesn't make mistakes. Just as the lion does a lot by its mighty roar the corruptible man will fight for its own way by a boisterous roar of bravado and supposed confidence. The focus is on self as king instead of the people of the kingdom. So instead of showing the face of God as the royal lion that is secure and righteous in its kingdom, the lesser face is that of the corruptible man, who creates his own righteousness and kingdom. One interesting point about the lion of the tribe of Judah is that when John sees Him in the book of Revelation chapter five, he sees the lion as the lamb who is worthy to open the scroll and break the seals. The elder who is in heaven sees the lion of the tribe of Judah, but John sees the lamb standing as if slain. This is a good image of how the lion is also identical with the lamb who still stands even as if it was slain. This is a great challenge to the corruptible man. There is no place for pride and self-glory when you must stand as a sacrificial animal that has been slain. The perfect man that is corrupt can't stand as a slain sacrifice. He will fight to stand in self-glory to prove he can't be slain. In the midst of challenges that the lion faces, the choice will be to compete with kingdoms of men or stand as the lion in the true kingdom that has overcome as a lamb slain.

Confrontation

How does one confront a lion? This may seem like a daunting task and it certainly is. I am sure that you have had to deal with people that carry the face of the lion. The lion is the king of the jungle. When we have to face someone who is the lion who might be veering off course, the way to help them is to focus on the kingdom. To focus on the right kingdom is to help them to be reminded of who they are and what the purpose is that they are trying to accomplish. This means that we can appeal to them on the basis of which battles should be fought and on which battlefields. If we can help to call them to the right battles and battlefields, we can help them to be who they are according to God's glory and not the corruptible man. They will not be as successful or productive in their identity if they directly fight everything that challenges them. God is the one who will handle the other kingdoms.

Genealogy

The genealogy of Jesus in the gospel of Matthew starts with an introduction of three identifying titles. The first is Jesus is the Messiah. Jesus is the Christ. He is the anointed one. The Messiah is the one chosen to rule. He is the king. This opening identification is the biggest declaration that could be made of someone. The Messiah is to set up the kingdom of God in perfect peace and prosperity. The Messiah is a perfect teacher of the law, able to build the temple of God. He will rule over all with kindness and be able to bring unity to man. This is the lion, the true king of all kings. Secondly, as king, He is the son of David confirming the requirement of the bloodline that God had chosen, as well as fulfilling the promises to David of his descendants. Thirdly, He is the son of Abraham, the one chosen and called out by God as His own inheritance. Abraham is recognized as the father of the Hebrew people. As Abraham was the progenitor of the nation of God, it is fitting that Jesus' genealogy would go all the way back to the first man of the nation. As Matthew begins with these three titles, he is saying that Jesus the Messiah has the full backing and weight of the promises of God. The king is here. The lion is on the scene and in the full royalty and regalia of his identity. The genealogy starts with Abraham and goes all the way to Joseph, the husband of Mary. This genealogy descends from Abraham to Jesus, the kingly descendant. The list is shared through the phrase "the father of." The Father has given the son and sets in place the king. Then, to conclude the list of genealogy, he is once again called the Messiah bookending the list with the main point of listing the genealogy. In verse seventeen of chapter one we are told of the breakdown of fourteen generations from Abraham to David, David to the Babylon deportation, the Babylon deportation to the Messiah. The story of the nation identified by Abraham, David, and the Messiah. The breakdown of 14 generations can be a hint to the reality of Passover that was to be observed on the 14th day of the first month. Maybe in Matthew's listing of the genealogy he is hinting at the Messiah being tied to the Passover. Fourteen multiplied by three equals forty-two. Forty-two divided by seven equals six, placing Jesus the Messiah at the start of the seventh seven. There are also forty names that the lineage goes through with Jesus being the forty-first. Forty is a well-known number in the scriptures usually connected to trial, testing, and a journey of transformation. With the forty names complete Jesus is also the beginning of the promise land reign.

In this genealogy, Matthew includes four women before we get to Mary by whom Jesus was born. Matthew's identifying of these four women is a key to redemption. It is the lion that identifies the lionesses in the line of Jesus. The four women were all between Abraham and David, the first set of fourteen. The women were Tamar, Rahab, Ruth, and Bathsheba. We will look at each woman in the redemptive woman section. The four women also shared the reality of being Gentiles. These women hinted that the Messiah includes those from outside into the king's royal family.

Notes

After the genealogy, the gospel begins to tell of Jesus' conception, birth, and childhood. In this gospel the angel of the Lord appears to Joseph in a dream and gives him instructions and prophecy. It is Joseph that is emphasized to show the reality of the kingly lion. In verse 20 of chapter 1, the angel addresses Joseph as "the son of David". This not only ties back to the genealogy but reminds Joseph of his identity in the line of the king. Joseph is going to have to make some decisions and lead his family. In Matthew, the angel's name is not mentioned as Gabriel, just that he is of the Lord. This angel would continue to come to Joseph in dreams telling him to, "Get up! Take the Child and His mother and flee to Egypt..." (2:13 NASB) and "Get up, take the Child and His mother, and go into the land of Israel..." (2:20 NASB). The perspective of God's leading is through that of Joseph, son of David.

In the beginning of Jesus' story, we quickly find one of the kingdoms that desires to destroy him. It is only in Matthew that the story of Herod and the magi are found. The magi come to Jerusalem in search of the King of the Jews. The star is called "His star" and the magi have come to worship him. When the magi arrive and inquire where the King of the Jews is, Herod hears of this and is troubled with all of Jerusalem (v2). Herod gathers all the chief priests and scribes to learn where this king will be born (v3). These are being identified as some of the first kingdoms that will be set against the true king. The magi, being sent out by Herod, find the Child not in the manger but in a house. In the house, they prostrate themselves and worshipped him. Then they give to him the gifts for a king: gold, frankincense, and myrrh. What the magi do and the gifts they give stir in us the importance of the Child. It is only for the king that these magi travel with kingly gifts, and then in seeing the king and worshipping him they are warned in a dream not to return to Herod. The worldly kingdoms will be dealt with, and it is God who does the dealing. Jesus, the child, the king of the Jews, doesn't try to fight Herod in his own kingdom according to his laws. God orchestrates the life of the king, and the worldly kingdoms are dealt with. The entire beginning of Matthew begins with a roar of the lion. The regal king had come to save His people from their sins establishing the true kingdom.

Jesus' first recorded teaching in Matthew is the sermon on the Mount where He began with the beatitudes. Jesus began by identifying the blessed, which means "well off" or "fortunate". The list of those who are blessed is not what the worldly kingdoms would identify as blessed people, but I believe Jesus is starting His teaching by identifying those who are a part of the true kingdom of which He is the king. This is a roar from the mountain to those who belong to the true kingdom. Mountains speak of power, government, royalty, authority, and the theme of mountains will continue to be the backdrop of the work of the king. Mountains are talked about in the other gospels but not as much as Matthew. Unique to Matthew, in the last temptation of Jesus Satan takes Him up on a very high mountain (4:8), healings of crowds and feeding of more than four thousand take place on the mountain (5:29-38). Mountains mark the beginning of Jesus' recorded teaching and the release of the disciples at the end of Matthew. Mountains are important in Matthew because this is where the king governs. The true king and His kingdom are tied to mountains because His government has no end and no equal that goes forth from Mount Zion, where David reigned. Mount Zion is the dwelling of the royal king. The true king is comfortable on mountains, often sitting and praying; it is His true dominion.

The Messiah, who is to rule in righteousness, is going to fulfill prophecies. This is the line of thought the Jews would rightly have and even the earthly kings would pay attention to, as we saw with Herod. Matthew uses the word "righteousness" more than any of the gospel writers. It is mentioned six times compared to one in Luke, zero in Mark and two in John. Jesus in his sermon on the mount said, "Think not that I am come to destroy the law, or the prophets: I am not come to destroy, but to fulfill" (5:17 KJV). This is the biggest claim to righteousness that could be made. When Jesus goes to John to be baptized, John tries to prevent this from happening on the basis that it should be the other way around. Jesus tells him to allow it based on fulfilling all righteousness, thus John relents (3:15). This is the first mention in Matthew of righteousness. Four mentions of righteousness are found in Jesus' sermon on the mount (5:6, 10, 20) including the well-known line of "seek ye first the kingdom of God, and his righteousness; and all these things shall be added unto you" (6:33 KJV). The last mention of righteousness is when Jesus speaks of John saying, "For John came unto you in the way of righteousness, and ye believed him not: but the publicans and the harlots believed him: and ye, when ye had seen it, repented not afterward, that ye might believe him" (21:32 KJV). The way of righteousness that John came in is the way that Jesus fulfills and says that to be a part of His way and kingdom you must believe. The people of His kingdom are those whom He saves from their sins when they believe. Another phrase that Matthew uses showing how Jesus kept His word in the sermon on the mount is "fulfill what was spoken by(through) the prophet". This phrase is used ten times to introduce a prophecy and possibly an eleventh time depending on translation. The prophecies include: the virgin birth of Immanuel (1:22-23), out of Egypt the Son is called (2:15), death of the infants (2:17-18), called a Nazarene (2:23), great light in Galilee (4:14-16), He taking our infirmities and disease (8:17), His ministry (12:17-21), parables (13:35), the king on an ass and colt (21:4-5), and the 30 pieces of silver for the potters field (27:9-10). The eleventh use of the phrase is about them casting lots for his garment (27:35), from Psalm 22, and is not included in some translations. Righteousness and fulfilling prophecies are the life of the Messiah. This lion is perfect and the ways of His life and kingdom fulfill who God is and what God says.

The righteous king is worthy of being worshipped. In Matthew, we find the most examples of people worshipping Jesus. We saw that the magi worshipped Him as a child. He was also worshipped by a wide variety of people. He was worshipped by a leper (8:2), and He is worshipped by a synagogue official (9:18). Both examples are before their request for healing. This is also the case with the Canaanite woman whose daughter is demon possessed. The woman calls Jesus the "Son of David" and receives the healing after her reply of faith to Jesus, implying she was a dog (15:22-28). The disciples are also recorded worshipping Him three times, once in the scene of Jesus and Peter walking on water (14:33), and then twice after Jesus' resurrection (28:9,17).

Matthew is the only gospel that uses the phrase "kingdom of Heaven" and "church". Church is used in the book of Acts but not in Luke's gospel. People argue both ways in the debate of the kingdom of

Heaven and the kingdom of God being the same thing, but, regardless of where you land, the fact is still that Matthew is the one to use "kingdom of Heaven". The kingdom of Heaven does point to a kingdom that is not of this earth or subject to the kingdoms of this earth, so the phrase still fits the face that Matthew is showing of Jesus. The territory and dominion of the kingdom of Heaven is real however you may define its bounds. The authority that the king has is evident. The church is part of the king's kingdom. In Matthew, we get a glimpse of some of the tactic and weaponry that the kingly lion has. In Peter's confession of Jesus being the Christ, the Son of the living God, it is only Matthew that includes verses 17-19, "And Jesus answered and said unto him, Blessed art thou, Simon Barjona: for flesh and blood hath not revealed it unto thee, but my Father which is in heaven. And I say also unto thee, That thou art Peter, and upon this rock I will build my church; and the gates of hell shall not prevail against it. And I will give unto thee the keys of the kingdom of heaven: and whatsoever thou shalt bind on earth shall be bound in heaven: and whatsoever thou shalt loose on earth shall be loosed in heaven" (KJV). Wow, this sounds like a pronouncement of war. Gates of Hades, which are defensive structures, not overpowering the church, and keys to the kingdom that have to do with binding and loosing on earth and heaven all point to a reality of victory for the king and His kingdom. Given the fact that Jesus said this in the district of Caesarea, Philippi also factors into the weight of His words. This area was also the place of Mount Hermon, which some believe is where the fallen beings that rebelled against God descended and wreaked havoc in the Genesis narrative. So, this is a huge statement with implications of how the true king has come to save

His people and deal with all the false kingdoms that have tried to come against God. As a bonus, Matthew informs us that Jesus has at His disposal from the Father more than 12 legions of angels (26:53).

Matthew shows flashes of how the lesser kingdoms are dealt with by providing some unique information on these lesser kingdoms and how to deal with them. In Chapter 2 Herod's plans fail as God speaks in dreams to the Magi and Joseph. In chapter 17:24-27 the two-drachma tax is paid with a coin in the fish's mouth after telling Peter that the sons are exempt from the poll tax. In chapter 22:15-22 the Pharisees try to trap Jesus concerning the poll tax and He explains based on whose likeness is on the coin how it should be rendered, to Caesar what is Caesar's and to God what is God's. In chapter 27 we find the most detail concerning Judas's death (v3-5), what the chief priests did with the blood money (v3-10), and that Pilates' wife had a dream and instructs Pilate to "have nothing to do with that righteous Man." Matthew also informs us that the guards were bribed to tell a certain story (28:12-15). These are not necessarily direct attacking strategies of earthly kingdoms, but they do hint at the workings of the true king towards the lesser kingdoms.

Judas

We already noted that Matthew gives us the details on how Judas died and that the money he had was used to buy the Potter's field by the chief priests. How Judas acquired the 30 pieces of silver is detailed that he made a bargain with the chief priests. Judas is the one who went to the chief priests. Judas is called one of the twelve showing that this attack on the king comes from within his own group. Matthew's account of Jesus' interaction concerning Judas begins as he comes to his disciples to tell them that "the hour is at hand the Son of Man is being betrayed into the hands of sinners" (26:45 KJV) while he was saying this Judas, once again called one of the twelve, shows up with a large crowd with swords and clubs. Here is the interaction:

> "And forthwith he came to Jesus, and said, Hail, master; and kissed him. And Jesus said unto him, Friend, wherefore art thou come? Then came they, and laid hands on Jesus and took him. And, behold, one of them which were with Jesus stretched out his hand, and drew his sword, and struck a servant of the high priest's, and smote off his ear. Then said Jesus unto him, Put up again thy sword into his place: for all they that take the sword shall perish with the sword. Thinkest thou that I cannot now pray to my Father, and he shall presently give me more than twelve legions of angels? But how then shall the scriptures be fulfilled, that thus it must be? In that same hour said Jesus to the multitudes, Are ye come out as against a thief with swords and staves for to take me? I sat daily with you teaching in the temple, and ye laid no hold on me. But all this was done, that the scriptures of the prophets might be fulfilled. Then all the disciples forsook him, and fled (26:49-56, KJV)."

The themes in this interaction point out the battle. There is a crowd with swords and clubs, but Jesus doesn't take the bait of fighting physically. God's orchestration is at work. Judas addresses Jesus as Hail Rabbi and kisses Him. Hail is a joyful salutation, and Rabbi in Hebrew means "master". Was this Matthew's way of showing that even Judas is ignorant of how this moment would start the process for great rejoicing of the Master, or was it Judas mocking who Jesus truly is? Jesus responds to Judas not in a fighting way but addresses Him as "friend". I think this is Jesus keeping Judas on a level that is under that of kingship and not responding to him on a basis of being a king. Naturally, kings would and should have ordered for the head of the betrayer to be swiftly removed, but not Jesus. Jesus gives a swift rebuke to His disciple, Peter, who draws a sword and removes the ear of the high priest's slave. The words of Jesus that "those who take up the sword shall die by the sword" are revealing that Jesus' way of fighting the betrayer is not by the sword. Jesus doesn't need a physical defense from his disciple; He could call the 12 legions of angels. To conclude, Matthew gives us the line of fulfilling what was spoken by the prophets. God is showing that the enemies of the king will be used to fulfill what God has already spoken of His perfect plan of redemption.

How does the lion deal with betrayal and the betrayer? I think the emphasis comes down to asking what the exact cost is. Matthew emphasizes the cost. Thirty pieces of silver, buying the potter's field, twelve legions of angels and living and dying by the sword all point to different costs in a kingdom. The areas of cost are currency, land, armies, and life itself. The person that carries the face of the lion will be tempted to fight back out of pride and defensiveness. The true response of the lion is to respond how Jesus does by acknowledging that God's plans are still being carried out and that nothing shall pull him away from that. Jesus sees the true cost of what is at stake and will not lose focus on the fulfillment and establishment of the true kingdom, even if that means he is arrested and lays down his life. By counting the cost, the king can make the wise decision for the kingdom and not fall prey to the folly of fighting Judas. Judas is not the enemy. Jesus keeps him on a friend level of communication, not addressing him as some kingly power, for even he will be used to bring about the fulfillment of the plan.

The Redemptive Woman

The redemptive women are found in the genealogy of Jesus that Matthew list. Why did Matthew include these four women? Matthew is the face of the lion, the king of the kingdom. When we start to mature and take on the face of the lion, we know that there are areas and decisions that the king can be challenged to overreact and become hot-tempered about. We know that kings are powerful, but they often need to be reminded of their own word and to make sure that their power doesn't start to blind them to their responsibility or focus. I think Matthew, showing the face of the lion, was aware of the temptation of the king to become drunk with power. So, he included these redemptive women that apply to each gospel. This foreshadows that a true king will establish redemptive principles in the kingdom so that it retains its health and vitality. The principal of salvation through redemptive birthing is what God said of the woman's seed in Genesis 3:15. I think this is what Paul was pointing to in his first letter to Timothy where he says, "Notwithstanding she shall be saved in childbearing, if they continue in faith and charity and holiness with sobriety" (2:14 KJV). Matthew's genealogy includes Tamar, Rahab, Ruth, and Bathsheba. Each of these women were incredible in what they did to bring forth redemption. Let's look at the first one Tamar that parallels the lion.

The first woman in the genealogy of the Messiah is Tamar. Tamar's story is found in Genesis 38:

"Now Judah took a wife for Er his firstborn, and her name was Tamar. But Er, Judah's firstborn, was evil in the sight of the Lord, so the Lord took his life. Then Judah said to Onan, "Go in to your brother's wife, and perform your duty as a brother-in-law to her, and raise up offspring for your brother." Onan knew that the offspring would not be his; so when he went in to his brother's wife, he wasted his seed on the ground in order not to give offspring to his brother. But what he did was displeasing in the sight of the Lord; so He took his life also. Then Judah said to his daughter-in-law Tamar, "Remain a widow in your father's house until my son Shelah grows up;" for he thought, "I am afraid that he too may die like his brothers." So Tamar went and lived in her father's house. Now after a considerable time Shua's daughter, the wife of Judah, died; and when the time of mourning was ended, Judah went up to his sheepshearers at Timnah, he and his friend Hirah the Adullamite. It was told to Tamar, "Behold, your father-in-law is going up to Timnah to shear his sheep." So she removed her widow's garments and covered herself with a veil, and wrapped herself, and sat in the gateway of Enaim, which is on the road to Timnah; for she saw that Shelah had grown up, and she had not been given to him as a wife. When Judah saw her, he thought she was a harlot, for she had covered her face. So he turned aside to her by the road, and said, "Here now, let me come in to you"; for he did not know that she was his daughter-in-law. And she said, 'What will you give me, that you may come in to me?' He said, therefore, 'I will send you a young goat from the flock.' She said, moreover, 'Will you give a pledge until you send it?' He said, 'What pledge shall I give you?' And she said, 'Your seal and your cord, and your staff that is in your hand.' So he gave them to her and went in to her, and she conceived by him. Then she arose and departed, and removed her veil and put on her widow's garments. When Judah sent the young goat by his friend the Adullamite, to receive the pledge from the woman's hand, he did not find her. He asked the men of her place, saying, 'Where is the temple prostitute who was by the road at Enaim?' But they said, 'There has been no temple prostitute here.' So he returned to Judah, and said, 'I did not find her;' and furthermore, the men of the place said, 'There has been no temple prostitute here.' Then Judah said, 'Let her keep them, otherwise we will become a laughingstock. After all, I sent this young goat, but you did not find her.' Now it was about three months later that Judah was informed, 'Your daughter-in-law Tamar has played the harlot, and behold, she is also with child by harlotry.' Then Judah said, 'Bring her out and let her be burned!' It was while she was being brought out that she sent to her father-in-law, saying, 'I am with child by the man to whom these things belong.' And she said, 'Please examine and see, whose signet ring and cords and staff are these?' Judah recognized them, and said, 'She is more righteous than I, inasmuch as I did not give her to my son Shelah.' And he did not have relations with her again" (NASB).

Tamar's story is one of courage. Tamar had a rough pick for a husband in Judah's firstborn Er. He was evil so the Lord took his life. This continued with Er's brother when he was to take her and produce an offspring. Eventually, Judah's wife dies, and he is in mourning. Judah had not kept his word concerning his son Shelah. Tamar decides to give up her garment of mourning as a widow and take action so that she can give birth to a child. Judah, in his mourning, decided to have intimate relations with a harlot. This harlot was Tamar. It was not known to Judah that it was Tamar because she covered herself with a veil. Tamar didn't just allow Judah to do what he wanted, but she made a deal with him to ensure that his word would be kept. Judah had pledged a goat which was the payment for a temple prostitute. Judah didn't have the young goat with him, so Tamar laid out the terms for Judah to give his seal, his cord, and his staff. These three items of Judah may not have had that much value on their own but to Judah, they would have been of immense value. They speak to his authority, kingship, ability to work his territory and exercise dominion in his life. Judah recognizes that to make a scene about these things would cause him to become a laughingstock. So, when Judah keeps his word and sends the young goat as payment to her, she is not found. When Judah finds out that Tamar is pregnant, he thinks that she should be burnt. This is revealing about Judah's strength and authority. It is his word that has power. This is the very thing that is recognized by Tamar and acted upon.

Tamar planned based on the authority of Judah's word. When Tamar is confronted, she responds to

Judah by showing him the three items that belonged to the father of the child. Judah recognizes that they are his seal, cord, and staff. Tamar didn't confront him directly and accuse him of not fulfilling his word. She didn't speak negatively of him. Tamar allowed Judah's own authority to be the tool by which she confronted him. She allowed his word and actions to remind him of himself. This is redemption for Judah, Tamar, and the children Perez and Zerah. Tamar brought forth redemption through authority. Authority is how you speak to authority. Tamar didn't have authority based on herself but based on the authority of Judah's own word. After Tamar presents Judah's own authority back to him, through the three items, Judah reveals the reality of Tamar's life. Judah says that Tamar "is more righteous than I". What an affirmation that would be for Tamar. Judah is reminded of his own word, action, and authority. Tamar reveals redemption through authority. She risked her life so that the authority of Judah could continue, and the authority of his firstborn son would continue. She didn't make a claim based on self. She birthed redemption through the means of proper authority. This is what the lion needs when he forgets his word, action, or authority. The lion knows the sound of a roar and can recognize his own roar. When redemption is needed in the life of one who has the face of the lion, an appeal and reminder of true authority is the way to redeem. For the lion, Tamar shows redemption through authority.

End of the Gospel

The end of Matthew's gospel finishes with a bang. The King has risen. The last chapter of the story in Matthew begins with the two Marys that came to the tomb. When they arrived, they encountered an angel of the Lord. This angel of the Lord had descended from heaven and there was a severe earthquake. This would have been the second shaking of the earth. The earth shook also when Jesus yielded up His spirit and the veil of the temple was rent in two (27:50-51). This angel of the Lord had the appearance of lightning with clothes that were white as snow. This angel of the Lord comes like a powerful royal herald. The angel's presence was so awesome that the guards shook for fear and became like dead men (28:1-4). This is a powerful scene that speaks to the dominion and the authority of the true king that has overcome the grave. The king that has risen has a heavenly herald, but he does not appear at the tomb. It says that they left the tomb quickly and then Jesus met them and greeted them (28:8-9). Why would Matthew record that Jesus meeting them was after they had left the tomb? I think this is the face of the lion that has overcome. Matthew is showing that Jesus is no longer connected to the grave, and the tomb is a reality that has been overcome. The king will no longer be connected to the grave. The king will meet with his disciples on the mountain. Between the first and last part of chapter 28 Matthew tells the story of how the guards are bribed by the chief priests to say that Jesus' body was stolen while the guards were asleep. The chief priests also assure the guards that they will be able to handle the governor should he hear of this fabricated story that the guards would be reprimanded for. This sandwich of victory for the lion shows how Matthew's focus is on the kingdom of the true king. The lesser kingdoms are made to feel like a side note that isn't that important but still worthy of mentioning how they will try to manipulate to maintain power.

The ending of chapter 28 is the commissioning of the disciples that most Christians are familiar with and is the evangelistic motivator of the church. This last scene incorporates all the themes of the kingly lion who has come to save His people from their sins, establishing His kingdom in true righteousness. The kingly commission isn't in the form of a dictate of power to conquer by force but to go forth in the same way that Jesus the true lion has gone forth in Matthew.

> "Then the eleven disciples went away into Galilee, into a mountain where Jesus had appointed them. And when they saw him, they worshipped him: but some doubted. And Jesus came and spake unto them, saying, All power is given unto me in heaven and in earth. Go ye therefore, and teach all nations, baptizing them in the name of the Father, and of the Son, and of the Holy Ghost: Teaching them to observe all things whatsoever I have commanded you: and, lo, I am with you always, even unto the end of the world. Amen" (28:16-20 KJV).

The eleven disciples are gathered in their obedience to their king and savior. They have yet to see Him since His resurrection, but still obey him and go to the mountain that He designated. When they do see Him, they worship Him. They worship even though some of them were doubtful. In the kingly setting, obedience and worship is important even in the midst of doubt. In the execution of a kingdom, we may doubt but we should not allow that doubt to stop us from following the order of the king. Jesus' first words don't address their doubts or questions. His first words as the resurrected king are about royal power and kingdom. All authority has been given to Him in the territory of heaven and earth. This is the king, on the mountain, alive and now releasing the kingly decree for His disciples. The decree to them is based on these first words of all authority being given to Him. The authority that the disciples have is not found in themselves but in the king that is commissioning them. Jesus continues, "Go therefore and make disciples of all nations..." There is no request or option. The "go" is a comand. Making disciples isn't about asking for volunteers or marketing promotions to gain followers. Making disciples all comes down, not to force, but to the reality of living how Jesus lived – consistent relationship with God. That is the way of the lion: make learners, those who will follow the king in His kingdom. Jesus' commission is not limited to the territory of Galilee or even Israel. The territory of the kingdom will make disciples of all nations. I used to wonder why Jesus didn't say make disciples of people. His use of nations shows that all nations are subject to the true king and kingdom. I think Jesus using the word "nations" is revealing and hints back to the reality that the nations were given their inheritance and the boundaries of the people were set (Deut. 32:8). The authority is of all heaven and earth and so the commission speaks to the full redemptive plan of God of all heaven and earth. The disciples are to be baptized and taught to observe all that the eleven were commanded. This is the reality of righteousness. Jesus is stating the standard of God in this commission. Jesus then concludes with the reminder that He is with them "always even unto the end of the world." Much could be said, but the emphasis is on the presence of the king always present with them.

The end of this gospel shows the restoration and establishment of the true king and His kingdom. He is positioned and poised as king of the kingdom. Not only has the Messiah come who rules righteously, but His reign has begun and those of His kingdom are now commissioned to go. The eternal king is ever-present. This is the face of the lion. God has been revealed. When we see him, we shall be like him.

CHAPTER 8

THE OX

The second face of God is that of the ox. The gospel of Mark reveals the face of the ox. The writer of the gospel of Mark is identified as an interpreter of Peter and could have been the John Mark referenced in Acts 12 and 15. The major themes of Mark are sacrificial service, bearing burdens, true work, power, and a fast pace. Mark is the shortest of the gospels with most of his material also contained in Matthew and Luke. The ox is concerned with doing the things it's supposed to do. The ox is the animal of power and strength used to plow and pull. The ox is used to focus on his row and plow ahead under the direction of the plowman. The ox doesn't serve the ground it plows or the creation it changes; it serves its master. God is likened to the horns of the wild ox in Numbers 23:22. This reference is one of power through sacrifice because it was through Passover that they had deliverance. Mark tells the story of Jesus, the sacrificial servant of God, who gets to work doing what is to be done.

The Key

In chapter 1 Mark starts quickly. He is straight to

work. The key is in the fact that he starts quickly. Mark tells little of John then straight into Jesus' baptism, preaching, calling disciples, teaching, deliverance, and healing. All this in chapter one poses the question of how Jesus made His decisions of work. The first point of description of Jesus' personal time comes in verses 35-38:

> "And in the morning, rising up a great while before day, he went out, and departed into a solitary place, and there prayed. And Simon and they that were with him followed after him. And when they had found him, they said unto him, All men seek for thee. And he said unto them, Let us go into the next towns, that I may preach there also: for therefore came I forth" (KJV).

The key is in His personal time in secluded prayer. Prayer is how the ox is led because prayer yokes us with the will of the Father and the power of the Spirit. Out of His prayer, He is able to stay focused on the reason for His coming. In His prayer, He has relationship with the one who is leading Him. Jesus, the ox, did not come to serve man. Jesus is serving God and rendering service to man. Man is not leading the ox, it is God, and Jesus knows the direction to plow, through prayer. The key for the ox is to go, being led by God, rendering service to man. Others may join Him in this service, and this is what He calls them to. He says to His disciples, let us go somewhere else not being led by everyone who is looking for Him.

The Challenge

The challenge is seen in the same scripture as the key.

To have time in prayer with God, He wakes early in the morning while it is still dark. He must depart into that solitary place. He has already done a lot of work. So, the challenge isn't at the start of the work as much as it is in the continuing of the work. The challenge is to maintain His time of prayer with God where God directs Him so that He isn't overworked by doing the things that God isn't directing Him to. All men seek for Jesus the ox, the one who is the sacrificing servant of God. That is a heavy load. Jesus chooses not to follow the voice of man but God. The ox needs time in his stall alone, often in the dark. This is where his strength comes from and where he has true rest. Notice that when Jesus goes in the direction that He is to go, He doesn't try to prove why He is doing what He is doing. The challenge of the ox is answered with a paradox of true rest in time of prayer with God, but if He doesn't have the direction of God there is a lesser image that He will take on.

Lesser Image of glory

The lesser image the ox will exchange for, is that of the birds. The birds are those that fly above and represent pseudo higher knowledge. There are good birds, but the negative sense of birds is that they pick at things. Satan is compared to the birds of the air that snatch away the seed that is sown (Mark 4:4,15). The lesser image goes from the glory of the ox with power, strength, and perseverance, to that of the bird that will try to prove its correctness by facts and knowledge. The lesser form will appeal to data, facts, information as the basis for action. It isn't that those things are bad, but that is not the purpose of the ox. The sacrificial ox isn't there to prove by facts and knowledge; he is there to plow. This is some of the reason why Mark doesn't provide so many details of Jesus' story and teachings. When the ox exchanges the glory of God for the image of the bird informational proof becomes the basis of his action instead of being led by God. This will also come out against those who come against him in conflict. The ox is powerful and purposeful. When the ox is challenged the choice of response is between persevering in what God is saying to do and stopping to prove something or convincing them by some higher knowledge. The bird will pick at the seed that is sown trying to remove that sole focus of God's purpose being accomplished. The sacrificial ox is there serving God and rendering service to man. The ox should not take on that form of the birds that try to prove to man that they are correct as if man is the one who directs the ox. Challenges come, choices must be made, but the ox isn't meant to be a bird in the air. Serve God and go as He directs.

Confrontation

How do you confront the ox that has veered off course? To confront the ox, you recognize that his true power is in serving and you don't try to stop him from serving. You don't just tell him to stop working. That isn't appealing to the ox. The ox needs direct confrontation that calls them to the correct yoke. The ox wears the yoke but if he has taken on the wrong yoke and is being directed by the wrong master it becomes a tiring and frustrating life. The yoke for the ox is to be directed by God, not man. Man will try to put many yokes on the ox, but to confront him and have success, you should help them to identify what the yoke of God is for him. Don't try to prove your point or put some bridle in his mouth. Call those who have the face of the ox to the true sacrifice that God has called them to. If they don't know what that is, then they need to spend some time with God in prayer. The ox needs times that are restful and refreshing. These times don't usually come in the commotion of daily activity but in times of specific nonwork. The ox is known at times to kick against the goads. This isn't a bad thing. When the ox kicks against the goads, let them kick. Don't get in the way of their kick and don't remove the yoke that God has given them either. Their kicking is a reminder of the direction to go forward with their service. Pure service requires joy in life and the ox/calf will need time to jump around and skip. The ox knows the work of laying down its life and serving through hard soils. Help the ox/calf by allowing for times of joy and skipping around so that they aren't being over worked even if they are the ones coercing themselves to overwork. To confront the ox, it comes down to giving it to them straight, calling them to the correct yoke and sacrifice with some allowance for them to kick and jump.

Genealogy

The opening of Mark contains no genealogy. Mark opens with, "The beginning of the gospel of Jesus Christ, the Son of God." The start is not concerned with bloodlines of connections to past persons. This is the beginning of the gospel, not the beginning of Jesus Christ. Jesus Christ is identified with the title of "Son of God," which is used here and not again until Jesus has died. The genealogy of the gospel of Jesus Christ is through the work of Isaiah, the prophet, and John's work that has gone before Him. There is no mention of Jesus' parents or birth story. Jesus Christ is the Son of God. Outside of this, the ox doesn't have a genealogy.

Notes

Mark has the least amount of material in his gospel and also has the least number of notes in this book. The gospel is probably the most fast-paced out of the four, which is seen in Mark's language. The word "*eutheos*" is used in Mark more than any other gospel and is translated as "immediately, at once or straightaway". This word indicates how Mark transitions between Jesus' service. This language is fitting for the ox that plows. The transitions flow from act to act in a language that shows the busyness of the sacrificial servant. The language gives the sense of urgency and the timing of now. This is true of the ox. The ox doesn't want to get involved in fluff or unnecessary information. The flow of Mark is about doing the work. Go and then go to the next thing. The start is straight into the service and sacrifice of the ox that covers a lot of ground and lists a lot of places that Jesus went.

The start of Jesus' ministry is marked by John being taken into custody and that Jesus came into Galilee preaching the gospel of God. This identification of preaching the gospel of God hints that His focus is on who He serves. The good news is not identified as the gospel of the kingdom, but the good news of God and that His kingdom is at hand. Jesus is identified in the first verse as the Son of God, by the writer, but it is not until the centurion, standing right in front of Him as He breathed His last breath, that a person in the story refers to Him with this title (Mark 15:39). The spirits knew Him as the Son of God, but they were silenced. No human calls Him the Son of God until the centurion and that is immediately after the veil of the temple rent from top to bottom. The sacrificial ox doesn't reveal

Himself as the Son of God. The ox isn't seen as the Son of God until the sacrifice is complete. This is true of the sacrificial servant. They are not recognized for who they truly are until the sacrifice is complete or the work is complete.

One verse that is unique to Mark and pertinent to a theme of the ox is chapter 2:27 which says, "And he said unto them, 'The sabbath was made for man, and not man for the sabbath.'" Rest is important for the ox and defining what true rest is, plays out in Mark. The sabbath is about true rest, but it doesn't mean that all work stops. God is still working the works of God. That work is to believe in Him whom He has sent (John 6:29). God is working even now. God believes in Jesus Christ whom He sent, the Holy Spirit whom He sent, and in you whom He has sent. Hallelujah! True rest, by relationship in prayer, is the position that the ox operates from and from which he is empowered. The sabbath was made for man. The sabbath is what starts us off on the right foot and in the right position.

The ox is unique in that it is the only face that changes in the listings in scripture. The three listings of the faces of the cherubim, living creatures, are found in Ezekiel and Revelation. In Ezekiel, there are two listings. Ezekiel has a vision in which he sees the cherubim at first calling them living creatures. In Ezekiel 1:10 each of the creatures had each of the four faces, with the order of the man, lion, ox, and eagle. In Ezekiel 10:14 each one has each of the four faces, with the order of the cherub, man, lion, and eagle. In Revelation 4:7 each creature only has one face, and the order is that of a lion, calf, man, and eagle. Some writers have used a different order to apply these faces to the gospel usually following the first order of Ezekiel 1. I think that when John sees the living creatures, they are more differentiated and that this serves the progression of change from under the sea of glass in Ezekiel, both mentions, to on top of the sea of glass. The sea of glass is how the expanse is described and John mentions it in Revelation, being before the throne. The progression of the ox is to the cherub and then the calf. This progression of the face speaks to how the maturity of the ox plays out. The ox is an earthly servant picture that is grown, but that grows into more of a heavenly servant picture of the cherub. Then the ultimate is the purer form of the sacrificial calf. It could be that some of the reason that the unclean spirits recognized Jesus is that they could see the reality of that heavenly servant. Those on the earth couldn't see the Son of God revelation because they saw just a sacrificial ox, by the works preformed. It wasn't until the death of Jesus with the veil being torn that the humans could see the purity of the calf that was innocent.

The uniqueness of the ox reveals that those who have this face will have unique aspects to their lives that may not always be easy to see. The scriptures distinguish the progression to reveal what is often hidden about the ox face. The aspect of the cherub and calf face reveal strengths in the ox that can be overlooked. The cherub aspect of the ox shows that the ox will have a heavenly service awareness in them. The cherub being a more heavenly creature shows the reality of service beyond the limitations of material matters. Those who have the face of the ox will have an aspect of their lives that is deeply intuitive, mystical, and spiritual. They may not show this aspect or focus on it that much, but it is there inwardly. This cherub reality will often be a driving force in their lives and work even though it isn't seen outwardly.

The same is true of the calf aspect as of the cherub aspect. The calf aspect is that playful, joyful reality. The calf likes to have fun and have simplicity in their life. This aspect comes out in childlike things for the ox. People with the face of the ox will have things in their life that may look childish or seem opposite of the hardworking drive they have. The calf is pure and simple in its desire to skip and play. The ox has this calf aspect in their lives that is a reminder that work isn't everything and that God has an eternal youthfulness that abounds with joy.

Judas

In the face of the ox, Jesus faces betrayal in a unique way. Once again, as the key is seen indirectly by Jesus' action, the way to deal with the betrayer is seen in action not word. Judas immediately comes to Jesus, calls him "Rabbi" and kisses him. Jesus doesn't respond to Judas at all. Jesus doesn't respond to being called "Rabbi" or being kissed. What is the response of Jesus? Jesus' response is to give no response to Judas. Jesus is still serving according to God's plan. When the ox deals with betrayal the proper response is to not respond to the instigator or get caught in some argument. To continue in the work of God is the key for the ox. Continuing in the service that God has called the ox to is the safeguard from work or problems that take away from the purpose of God. When the slave of the high priest's ear is cut off, Jesus continues in His service and gives no response to the slave or the actions of the "one" who did the cutting. Jesus doesn't heal the ear in this account or rebuke the one who cut the ear off. The dialogue of Jesus goes straight into the words concerning how they come for Him as a robber to fulfill the scriptures. The ox is serving God, so when betrayal comes the focus remains on serving God. The betrayer might seem like a worthy distraction, but he isn't. Betrayal is not enjoyable. Jesus doesn't become emotionless and cold to continue in His serving. Mark records that Jesus was distressed, troubled, and deeply grieved in Gethsemane as He prays. Dealing with betrayal could be a reason for some to change what they are doing, but in service to God, we must continue the course. To be focused in serving God doesn't mean that we kill parts of ourselves, become cold or become a nonperson presence. Jesus remains present in the situation and stays focused on what God is saying and doing in the situation. The ox's power is in persevering in what God has called him to do.

Mark includes two unique verses at the end of the betrayal account (14:51-52). They are about a young follower of Jesus who was only wearing a linen sheet when he was seized. When this young man was seized, he broke free escaping naked, leaving behind the linen sheet. There is much speculation about who this is. Most lean to the idea that this is John Mark who is thought to have written the gospel. It is definitely a unique and personal piece of information, but its significance isn't as clear. It could be a way of identifying that the author of the gospel has authority to write the gospel having specific unique information of what happened. It could be a signature of some sorts. I think that it does add validity to the account of the author because it is something that is personal and would be shaming to share. If the author had just heard of this incident, it would be hard to understand why it would be included as secondhand information. The linen sheet's significance is tied to the burial cloth of Jesus and maybe speaks to the purity of the sacrifice. I tend to think that the young man losing his linen sheet speaks to humanity as a whole losing its pure clothing and that Jesus, even in death, had a pure clothing that He had in the grave.

The Redemptive Woman

The redemptive woman that is tied to the ox is Rahab. Rahab's story is found in the book of Joshua chapter two. Here is a synopsis of the story: Rahab was a harlot in the city of Jericho. Joshua has sent two men as spies to view the land that they were going to conquer. Jericho was a fortified city and the king of Jericho heard that spies were coming to spy out the land. The two men found refuge in the house of Rahab, and she lied to the king to protect their lives by hiding them on the roof of her house. Rahab confesses to the men that she knows that the Lord has given the land into their hands and tells them that what the Lord did for them has caused them to be terrified. Rahab, after hearing all the things that God did for Israel, then acknowledges that the Lord their God is the God in heaven above and earth beneath. Rahab then sends the spies away after making a deal with them to save herself and her family when they return to capture the city. The deal centers on the scarlet cord that she must hang in her window. This is the same window that she let them escape by going down a rope and telling them about the men on the road that were sent out to track and kill them.

Rahab represents redemption through sacrifice. There is no genealogy given of Rahab in the story or where she married Salmon. Some argue that Rahab in Matthew is different from Rahab who hid the spies. The only thing unusual about this is that it would look like Matthew includes a woman in the genealogy without any significance. How would Matthew know of the woman and then include her if she wasn't a revered woman that would be known to the readers? It seems far-fetched that it is an unknown Rahab and not the Rahab of Jericho. An interesting note about Rahab is that her child is Boaz and Boaz was sensitive and receiving of Ruth. It makes sense that Boaz would act this way toward Ruth if his mother was once a harlot in Jericho. There is more on Ruth's story in the next chapter.

Rahab doesn't follow the voice of the king of Jericho and risks her life in doing so. She is serving God and rendering service to man. There isn't much about Rahab personally except that she was a harlot. This scarlet cord that she hung in the window is a key to the story. The word for this chord is *tiqvah*. This cord is the reality of hope and expectation. When she made the deal and hung this cord in the window, she was saying that her hope was in the faithfulness of the deal being honored. Hope is a cord that connects us to the life that we can't see at the moment we know death could be imminent. The cord is scarlet which speaks to blood and the redemption that sacrifice brings through blood. Rahab brings redemption for her entire family by risking her life. Her entire family and all they have is saved because of her decision to risk her life. Sacrifice is more about the risking of life than about dying. Sacrifice does sometimes result in death, but the value and honor of sacrifice is not in the death itself. The value and honor of sacrifice is in risking your life to the unknown, which could mean death. Jesus said, "Greater love hath no man than this, that a man lay down his life for his friends" (John 15:13 KJV). He doesn't say to die for your friends, but to lay down your life. It is an act of your will and a choice that is true sacrifice. Rahab doesn't die to save her family, but she does choose to lay down her life so that there is a hope of salvation for her and her family. She laid down her life in hope and this is why she represents redemption through sacrifice. This is the redemption of the ox. The ox sees redemption come to fruition by a choice to lay down and be willing to face whatever the one he serves calls him to.

End of the Gospel

The end of the Gospel of Mark is one that has some debate about where the text ends. It is now considered that the end of Mark's gospel concludes with verse eight of chapter sixteen. Verses nine through twenty are believed to be added to the text to soften the abrupt ending of fear and trembling after seeing the empty tomb. The evidence leans more on the side of the text being added to versus some Christians and manuscripts omitting a huge chunk of important scriptures. I believe that the text originally did not include verse nine through twenty, but both endings speak to the face of the ox. We will look at both endings and see how they illustrate the message of the ox.

The abrupt ending of Mark is in line with the sacrificial servant. When the work of the ox is over, there is not much else that needs to be said. Jesus had already told His disciples that He would meet them in Galilee after He had been raised (14:27-28). Jesus is plowing ahead at the end of the gospel. Jesus has served God as He was sent to do. He has fulfilled the reality of sacrifice through his death on the cross. The ending of the ox is that the disciples are told that they will see Jesus in Galilee. The ending is a commission of the obedience that the disciples are to walk in and remembering that they are serving God who has said He will meet them in Galilee. The start of Jesus' ministry was in Galilee and the start for the disciples is Galilee where Jesus said he would meet them. Their work will continue serving God and rendering service to man. This is the face of the ox so let's go, for when we see Him, we shall be like Him.

The additional text is believed to come from tradition. I don't think that it was a part of the original text, but however the addition came to be included, it does speak and follow in line with the face of the ox. I also think that it should be included in our bibles with a footnote that gives some explanation of the discrepancy. The addition adds a nice touch to themes of Mark and gives a picture that work is done from a position of rest. The theme of rest and power is emphasized with a list of the signs that will accompany those who believe. The more formal commission is to go into the world and preach the gospel to all creation. The proclamation of the gospel is directed to all of creation, not the nations as we saw in Matthew. All creation is to be changed by the servants of God. Jesus is received up into heaven with the imagery of an acceptable sacrifice that God has accepted. When Jesus is received up into heaven, He is seated at the right hand of God. The Lord, now seated, shows us the picture of work from the enthronement of God. To work while seated in the throne is a reality of rest that shows the redemption of Jesus' sacrifice. The Lord still worked with them as they were sent out confirming the work with signs. It should be noted that the signs or attesting miracles that followed them were not the works that they did. The signs were a result of the sacrifice they lived. The work that they were called to was that of believing and preaching to all of creation to believe.

CHAPTER 9

THE MAN

The face like that of the man. Luke is the face of the man. This isn't the corruptible man that is a lesser form of glory that the lion takes on. This is a true man. The picture of true humanity is seen through Luke's biography of Jesus. The face of the man reveals the themes of humanity, family, relationships, the body, and joy. The Gospel of Luke is the longest of the gospel narratives and its conclusion has a continuation into the book of Acts. We have the most stories in the Gospel of Luke with ample notes and details to reveal the face of the man. The writer is usually linked to Luke, the "beloved physician", mentioned in Colossians 4:14. Luke provides the most material and detail in his writings. Luke wrote this book specifically to one person: Theophilus. It is not known who Theophilus was or what his significance was to Luke. It is unique that Luke would write such a detailed account for one person. Theophilus means "lover of God", so it is likely Luke is writing specifically to the individual who is a lover of God. This would tie into the reality of the key for the man.

The Key

The key for Luke is the largest key in terms of different aspects that are involved. The key for the man is found in the first four verses of chapter one, and it is highlighted throughout the first three chapters. The phrases that show the key for the man are: "set forth in order", "most surely believed among us", "delivered to us", "eyewitnesses", "ministers of the word", "having perfect understanding of all things from the very first", "to write in order", and "certainty of those things wherein thou hast been instructed". These phrases found in the first four verses show the importance and seriousness of Luke's writing. The key is the relational integrity that enables him to be precise and specific about the order of details that reveal the story of Jesus. This is how the man operates. The man is concerned with details, truth, exactness, order, and an account from the beginning. Luke acknowledges that there are other accounts and is adding his account so that the instruction that the lover of God has received will be buttressed with the exact truth. Those who have the face of the man will follow this same pattern of giving an account with detail based on relationship. The key to the face of the man is shown in some key verses that Luke records for us. Part of relationships is peace among men of goodwill that gives glory to God, which the angel and heavenly host declare this before the shepherds now that the Savior, Christ the Lord is born (2:8-14). Relationships must develop, grow and be maintained. We find Jesus as the child continuing in subjection to his parents as He kept "increasing in wisdom, stature, and in favor with God and men" (2:40, 51-52).

Simeon made a revealing statement to Mary that was

prophetic of what the effect of the man's face is and how it will affect others. He said, "this child is set for the fall and rising again of many in Israel; and for a sign which shall be spoken against; Yea, a sword shall pierce through thy own soul also, that the thoughts of many hearts may be revealed" (KJV). This is a result of the face of man being revealed. When the face of the man is revealed, how he relates to people will have a profound effect on other people and there will be a revealing of what is in their hearts. This is a reality of true relationship that we see fully in Jesus. Relationships are a revealing of hearts between people, and the man of God is a sign of what God is doing in the midst of the people. Luke shows this in his gospel. He shows how the man Jesus, whose heart is seen, reveals what is in the heart of others. Luke gives us the most detail of people's names, stories, and lives as he reveals the face of the man.

The Challenge

We all know that when we have relationships, we face challenges. The challenge that the man faces is the weakness of belief. The weakness of belief is answering the question, "how?". There are a lot of questions in this gospel that are trying to work out the challenge of how. When Luke tells the story of the angel appearing to Zachariah, his response of John being born is, "how will I know this?" (1:18). It seems that if an angel of the Lord appeared to someone and told him that something was going to happen, there would not be a need for some sort of confirmation or explanation. Yet, we struggle with the "how". Mary struggles with the same question when the angel comes to tell her of the word of the Lord and that she will conceive and bear a son (1:34). This challenge is also why Luke writes so much in his account. Remember that he is writing so that the instruction that was received has certainty to it. The certainty of how things are going to work out is the challenge the man faces. When Zachariah asked, "how will I know this?", the angel revealed himself personally by name. It is the angel Gabriel who has come to him with the good news, but because of his unbelief, he is made silent, unable to speak (1:19-20). This silencing of man reveals the power that man's voice has. The voice of man is how we create and build. The reason for the silence was so that Zachariah would not build or create from unbelief. One of the greatest, if not the greatest power of man, is to speak beliefs. This part of the story recorded by Luke illustrates the importance of paying attention to what we speak because the spoken beliefs effect the relationships and callings of God in our lives.

Lesser Image of Glory

The temptation the man faces when challenged is to exchange the glory of God for the image of a four-footed beast. You may ask yourself why the face of the man would take on the four-footed beast instead of the image of the corruptible man. That is a fair question. When the man is challenged and finds himself pursuing a course of action that isn't God's leading, he will turn to that image of the beast. You may have heard someone say they "acted like an animal". That saying is probably truer than we realize. The four-footed beast is an animal that lives out of its own strength and determination. The man will turn to a competitive nature of a beast using brute force to overcome the challenge. Instead of being relational and pursuing peace with men, they will push and force their way upon the situation. Relational challenges create a temptation of force to be employed by men to achieve their way. The lesser form of glory for the man is that of the beast that will use the strength of self to achieve their own will.

This four-footed beast image that the man exchanges for is not the same as the ox that is a face of God. This beast is one that is not led by God rendering service to man but led by malevolence rendering service to self. The beast may try to deceive with an image of helping others or some societal desire, but the result will not be unto the glory of God but the glorification of self at the cost of others life.

Confrontation

To confront the man is not as taunting as the lion or ox yet can still be difficult. The face of the man does have more of a tendency to be receptive and listen to those that have relational standing in their life but that isn't a guarantee. To help the man get back on track and to affirm their identity of the man, we call them back to the value of relationships. They will be open to receiving a message that will clarify the questions of how. Details and facts that remind and reestablish connections will be helpful to the man. To show how things can be accomplished or changed with an appeal to a vision of better relationships will help the man get back on course of God's design. The reality of togetherness, family, commitment, and humanity are all reminders that will help to stimulate them to who they are. We must be careful that our actions are done from a position of genuine care and respect, or we run the risk of entrenching them further in the lesser form of competing as the beast. Call the man to the details and facts that will help them to see how and remind them of relationship.

Genealogy

The genealogy that Luke gives is the longest and he doesn't give it until after Jesus is baptized by John. The genealogy is found at the end of chapter three after we have already had the birth story of John and Jesus. The genealogy starts with an introduction of Jesus starting his ministry at the age of thirty. Luke's placement of the genealogy ties it to the purpose of showing that Jesus is the picture of true family and the fulfillment of relationship. Luke starts his genealogy with Jesus being the son of Joseph. This is an important distinction between Matthew who started with Abraham and worked down through the generations to Jesus. Luke starting with Jesus and ascending all the way back to Adam who is the son of God shows that Jesus' ministry will work redemption of relationships all the way back to Adam, God's son. This is the natural line of Jesus showing the man connected to the man all the way back to the first man. This genealogy runs through Joseph and there are three Joseph's in the list. Joseph means, "let him add" or "God has added". God has added to humanity the one who redeems humanity. The genealogy contains 77 names. The genealogy is not focusing on kingship or specific people that show qualification, but that the whole picture is seen and the whole family is included.

Notes

Luke gives the most detail, names, and stories of the life of Jesus and how he revealed the hearts of others. Luke's gospel tells Jesus' story, but it is often told in conjunction with the story of others. Luke begins his gospel with the story of John's birth being foretold to Zachariah. Zachariah is in the temple performing his priestly duty of burning incense when the angel of the Lord appears to him (1:9-11). It is Jesus' family that begins the face of the man. Luke gives details of the family relations of Jesus before telling of Jesus's story making a statement of the importance of relationship and family. The theme of relationship continues to be shown forth as Luke gives the most details about John and Jesus' birth and childhood. It's only Luke who details, in his investigation of the eyewitnesses, how Jesus' story impacted Mary, Joseph, Zacharias, Elizabeth, John, Simeon, and Anna with detail. The stories of these people are not written just to tell Jesus' impact but also include how they responded. The response of others is important to the man. The man cares about humanity, not just what he does for them, but how they respond in their natural lives.

In Luke, the birth of Jesus is told from Mary's perspective more than Joseph's. The angel of the Lord came to a virgin engaged to Joseph, who is associated with the descendants of David, but not titled as a son of David. The angel Gabriel came to Mary calling her "the favored one whom the Lord is with" (1:26-28). Mary went to visit Elizabeth and she was filled with the Spirit at the sound of Mary's greeting. Mary is the only person to refer to God as "my Savior" (1:47). This personalization of the Savior to an individual is common in our language today because we tend to personalize and lean toward an individual self-perspective. For Mary to be the one who knows the personal Savior is revealing of Luke's message that the man is deeply committed to personal relationship. There might be a tendency to dismiss this as typical of a mother with her son, but that doesn't explain why Luke would record this from a woman. For Mary, a woman to be identified as saying this brings in another thread of Jesus' story as the man. That thread is that women are valued and important to God and what he is doing in humanity. This thread continues in Luke as he records the women disciples of Jesus by name, Mary Magdalene, Joanna wife of Chuza, and Susanna (8:1-3). Luke's inclusion of women and their stories is not by accident; it is a purpose of God being revealed.

It is Mary who, when Jesus is born, wraps him in clothes and lays him in a manger because there was no room in the inn (2:7). This isn't the kingly scene of Jesus in the house with the Magi's gifts. This scene is that of humanity having to find refuge in an abode that is humble and not the normal place for a mother and baby. This scene is a picture of humanity who has lost its normal place to stay and must find refuge in a lesser abode. This is the same picture we find of the prodigal son, a story unique to Luke, who has squandered his inheritance and finds himself among the pigs. Thankfully, the story doesn't end in this position. The story of man is infused with joy amid hardship. In the manger, the shepherds find Jesus as the sign for the "good news of great joy" (2:8-20). The prodigal son returns home to joy and celebration of the father (15:11-32). Humanity is being inundated with joy, by Luke's emphasis, as Jesus the man is revealed. John the Baptist leapt in the womb for joy (1:44). The 70 disciples return from ministering with great joy and are told to rejoice because their names are recorded in heaven (10:1-20). The revelation of God's face as a man shines with divine bliss. Luke's gospel has the most emphasis on joy. I think GK Chesterton had it right when he wrote in *Orthodoxy* that, "Joy, which was the small publicity of the pagan, is the gigantic secret of the Christian." The joy of the Lord is our strength (Nehemiah 8:10). It was for the joy set before Jesus that he endured the cross (Hebrews 12:2). The joy of the Lord that was set before Jesus is that reality of full relationship with humanity in the fullness of God's intention. It makes a lot of sense that Luke's gospel is laden with joy as the man, Jesus, is here redeeming humanity. The word redemption is only found in Luke's gospel, which is the man restoring relationships, which is God's joy.

Jesus' ministry in Luke is preceded by John's ministry and the most information of his preaching is given. Luke's quotation of John's preaching fulfilling Isaiah's prophecy is the only reference that includes verses 4 and 5 of chapter 40. The included verses speak of the leveling of ravines, mountains, crooked, rough, and then that all flesh will see the salvation of God. That leveling is restoration of things that stop relationship and the presentation that all flesh will see the salvation of God. When Jesus begins his ministry in Galilee Luke records that Jesus read from the book of Isaiah quoting the prophecy that He is anointed to preach to the poor, release captives, recover sight for the blind, free the oppressed, and proclaim the favorable year of the Lord. Jesus identifies those who he is coming to, and that this prophecy is fulfilled in their hearing (4:15-21). Luke record's Jesus' ministry to the poor and rich more than any other gospel. Also, in Luke is where we see Jesus eating with sinners and the word "sinner" being used more than the other gospel writers (5:29-32, 19:1-10).

Another section of Jesus' ministry and life that

is filled with detail is in the telling of the crucifixion unique to the man. The man Jesus is declared innocent three times by Pilate (23:4,13,22). He is also declared innocent by Herod (23:15), the thief on the cross (23:41), and by the centurion, after Jesus breathed his last (23:47). The face of the man drives home the point that Jesus was innocent more than any other gospel. As Simon the Cyrene is seized to help carry the cross with Jesus, Jesus says to the daughters of Jerusalem to stop weeping for him and to weep for themselves and their children (23:26-28). Even on the cross, the man still ministers and cares for relationship. When Jesus is on the cross, we hear His words asking the Father to forgive because they do not know what they are doing (23:34). Jesus has a conversation with the other criminals and tells one of them that He will be with him in Paradise today (23:39-43). It is also noted that the crowds were there at the cross and that His acquaintances and the women saw what was happening (23:48-49). The cross that the man bears is not so heavy that he is not aware of humanity and the relationship of God and man being restored.

Judas

The face of the man confronts the betrayer, and he addresses the question of "how?". Before the betrayal of Jesus and His arrest, Luke gives us a heads up of the dynamic that is happening in Judas. While the Passover was being prepared Luke tells us that at the scheming of the chief priests and scribes that Satan entered Judas who was called Iscariot (22:3). It seems that Luke presents that once Satan entered Judas, Judas then goes to the chief priests and scribes (22:4). This explains some of the questions of how things happened and reveals the workings of Judas' decisions. To answer the "how" question is also the approach that Jesus takes when addressing Judas. When Judas shows up and is going to kiss Jesus, he confronts Judas saying, "Judas, betrayest thou the Son of man with a kiss?" (22:48 KJV). This is confrontation initiated by Jesus. Jesus doesn't allow for Satan to be the initiator in the conversation. In the account there is no record of Judas' words. Those with Jesus ask if they should act with the sword and one of them cuts off the slave's ear. Jesus tells them to stop, and in this account heals the slave's ear. Jesus is seen caring for the lowly slave of the chief priest amid betrayal.

So, the way that the man deals with betrayal and the betrayer is to recognize that there are other forces that have influence in the action and decision-making process of the betrayer. Also, the man looks at the "how" of betrayal and confronts based on the "how", not based on the person. Jesus didn't ask Judas how he could do this. Jesus confronts with a question that reveals the kiss was that of betrayal revealing that the intimacy of relationship can be used for wickedness. For the man to see the "how" is a key to acting to confront, instead of reacting to an effect of betrayal. The man should be careful not to allow the hearing of the betrayer's words. Remember Zachariah who was made mute so that his struggle to believe would not build something that wasn't of God? If the man gets caught up in hearing the words, he will often get bogged down in trying to answer them. The man must be the initiator when facing betrayal so that the "how" can be revealed with integrity and clarity of the situation.

The Redemptive Woman

The redemptive woman for Luke, the face of the man, is Ruth. Also, it is fitting that Ruth's story is not in a book of the Old Testament, but that she gets her own whole book. While we don't have enough space to discuss the entire book, we can point out some key points of her story that will illustrate how she is a picture of redemption. The whole book of Ruth is about the relationship that she had with Naomi, Naomi's family, Boaz, and then their child. Key decisions of relationship are what define Ruth. Ruth's story begins with the death of Naomi's husband who had taken his family to Moab during a famine. Naomi's sons found wives among the Moabites and Ruth was one of the wives. After ten years the sons died also so the story comes down to Naomi, Ruth and Orpah. When the sons die Ruth and Orpah face a decision at Naomi's push to return to their original families. At the behest of Naomi, Orpah does leave, but Ruth refuses to leave and stays with Naomi. Ruth's decision is to remain loyal to Naomi in her grief and loss. Ruth commits to Naomi, where she goes, where she stays, her people, her God, her death, and burial. That is a committed relationship. Naomi then sets in motion a plan for Ruth to be connected to Boaz who was the kinsman redeemer. Ruth goes and gleans in Boaz's field and Boaz allows her to do so with some instruction to stay close to his maids. Ruth takes some of her gleanings back to Naomi and Naomi gives her instruction on how to prepare herself for Boaz and how to engage him. Boaz and Ruth end up marrying. Ruth is compared to Rachel, Leah, and Tamar (4:11-12). The son that they have is laid in the lap of Naomi to be nursed, and his name is Obed, the grandfather of David

(4:16-17). Ruth is the redemptive woman that shows redemption through relationships.

End of Gospel

The end of Luke's gospel isn't really the end because he continues into the book of Acts. Luke ends his gospel with the themes of the man in full force. There are a lot of interactions that Jesus has with others after the resurrection. Jesus does a lot of explaining in these interactions. The book of Acts begins with Jesus explaining the kingdom for 40 days with convincing proofs with the disciples (Acts 1:3). In Luke's last chapter we find that two men, later called angels, are at the tomb when Mary Magdalene, Joanna, Mary of James, and other women arrive (24:4,10,23). On the road to Emmaus Jesus explains, to two men who are "slow of heart to believe (24:25)," all the scriptures about Himself from Moses to all the prophets. That would be a lot of detail in the full account of the Old Testament. Jesus then reclines with the two and breaks bread with them which opens their eyes to see Him (24:30). Then He appears to the disciples standing in their midst saying, "Peace to You" and asking them why they are "troubled" and have doubt arising in their hearts (24:26,28). Jesus explains the how to them through touch, sight, eating with them and then opens their minds to understand the scriptures (24:39-45). Jesus uses a key phrase of Luke telling His disciples that they are "witnesses of these things" (24:48) as He commissions them. The commission is that they are to stay "in the city of Jerusalem until ye be endued with power from on high" (24:49). Jesus does something that is the opposite of what He tells them to do because He leads them out to Bethany for His ascension (24:50).

Jesus leads them out to Bethany because that is where Mary, Martha and Lazarus were raised from the dead. Lazarus was raised physically but Mary and Martha were raised from the grave of unbelief. Jesus takes them out to Bethany to reveal that true relationship is based on resurrection life. In resurrection, we see the glory of God because we believed. So, the commission of the man is to be witnesses clothed with power from on high, praise and give glory to God, and to have relationships based on resurrection life. This is the face of God the man, and when we see Him, we shall be like Him.

CHAPTER 10

THE EAGLE

T he face like that of the flying eagle – the Gospel of John is the eagle. John's gospel is set apart from the synoptic gospels almost in the same way that the eagle is a creature of the air, not the land like the other three. It doesn't mean that the eagle doesn't touch the land but there is some distance between its abode and the abode of the other three faces. John's gospel illustrates the flying eagle that soars in the heights. The themes of the Gospel of John are eternity, divinity, and humanity in one, the earthly and heavenly together, sight, vision, and the cosmic scale. I believe the author of this gospel is John, the disciple who Jesus loved. In this gospel, we have the only identification of the writer by himself (21:24) and a directly written out purpose. The first three gospels are referred to as the synoptic gospels because they are said to give the same (syn) view (optic). John gives a different view, and the timing of his gospel is unique. Much of John's gospel is unique material that is revealing a different view of the story of Jesus. The eagle soars in the heights swoops down at specific times and can precisely grasp and reveal things.

The Key

The key for the eagle is to become flesh and dwell among humanity, full of grace and truth, that reveals the glory of the only begotten (1:14). The eagle could live distanced from others, satisfied in the eternal reality of relationship with God. While this is great, God calls the eagle to be the most incarnational. The eagle isn't just about revealing the heavenly or eternal things. The eagle is to reveal how eternity flows in temporality and how the heavenly is connected to the earthly so people will believe. The face of the eagle reveals and helps to explain God and His glory (1:18).

The purpose John gives for his gospel is that the signs "are written, that ye might believe that Jesus is the Christ, the Son of God; and that believing ye might have life through his name" (20:31). John is the only one who expressly writes his purpose in plain language even though he is the one that writes so mystically.

The Challenge

The challenge for the eagle is that the world does not know Him and those that are His own did not receive Him. This is a tough position to be in when you are trying to reveal the glory of God. Solomon writes that the way of the eagle in the sky is hard to understand (Proverbs 30:18-19). The world isn't going to receive God and His own people might reject the very reality they are looking for. The eagle is going to face a lot of skepticism. This comes with the territory of the heavenly and eternal in the midst of the earthly and temporal. His disciples will be found to be skeptical of why Jesus does certain things like when Jesus interacts with the

Samaritan woman (4:27). His brothers will not believe in Him and prod Him to act outside of His time to prove himself (7:1-9). Rejection, skepticism, and unbelief are challenges the eagle will face as He reveals the face of God. In the midst of challenges for the eagle, a caution would be to follow Jesus and not to entrust himself to man or need the testimony of man to confirm the identity of God (2:24-25). There is a fine balance that the eagle must navigate as He is to become flesh and dwell among the people full of grace and truth.

Lesser Image of Glory

The lesser form of glory that the eagle will exchange for is that of the image of a reptile. The reptile is also known as the "creeping things". In frustration, instead of flying like an eagle, the competitive position becomes that of the creature that creeps along the ground. The tactic of the reptile is to be sly and evasive. An eagle is a fragile animal in a way, and this is what allows the eagle to soar. When the eagle takes the image of the reptile there is an adoption of ground tactics to creep around staying hidden until the point of more assured victory. The image of the reptile is that he will present a part of himself but ultimately this is to draw in the competition to a position from which a deadly attack can be launched. Think of the crocodile or a scorpion and you can get a picture of the lesser image for the eagle.

Confrontation

Confronting the eagle can be one of the biggest challenges because eagles can fly above things in a way that makes them seem untouchable to a degree. When someone has the ability to soar above things and not come down into the middle of a situation it isn't likely to be persuaded by force or informational proof. To confront the eagle there must be a call to incarnation. A call to incarnation is a recognition of value and to help them see the present need that is being faced. A great way to help the process of incarnation is to ask questions that express a genuine desire to learn and grow. When the eagle is off course and disengaged from what God is doing, there has to be a presentation of need and a call to that identity of the eagle to help see and believe in hard times. The eagle has talons and a sharp beak that can pick things apart and be used to attack if confronted. This is the risk of trying to prove or convince the eagle of their wrong. Calling them to the vision God has given them and to dwell among the situation full of grace and truth is a safer and wiser course of confrontation.

Genealogy

The genealogy of the gospel of John fits the eagle so well. The genealogy doesn't focus on man or lineage of a king. The genealogy of Jesus in John is a genealogy of eternity. "Jesus Christ is the Word, in the beginning, with God, and was God" (1:1-2). The genealogy of Jesus Christ is eternal and everything that came into being got its genealogy through the Word (1:3). The Word became flesh. The genealogy of God is God.

Notes

John's vocabulary is set apart to emphasize the themes of the eagle. His language is intentional to draw the womb of your ear to receive and believe the Word who has become flesh. Look at some key words that

John uses. John uses the Greek word *kosmos*, (Strong's number G2889) 79 times compared to 9 in Matthew. The word truth (*aletheia* G225) is used 25 times compared to 3 in Mark and Luke. The word believe (*pisteuo* G4100) is used 100 times compared to 15 in Mark, while the word for faith (*pistis* G4102) is not found in John. The word Light (*phos* G5457) is used 23 times compared to 7 in Matthew. The word life (*zoe* G222) is used 36 times compared to 7 in Matthew. The words for love are also strongly unique in John. John uses love (*agape* G26), as a noun, 7 times compared to once in Matthew and Luke. John uses love (*agapao* G25) as a verb, 37 times compared to 13 in Luke. John uses love (*phileo* G5368), which is more of a brotherly love, 13 times compared to 5 in Matthew. John uses that mystical phrase that is the name of God, more than any other gospel writer. He writes I am (*ego eimi* G1473 G1510) 41 times, compared to 9 in Matthew and Luke. This phrase is a perfect fit for the eagle because you can't say God's name, "I Am", without including yourself. John's use of these words resounds in us to know God's nature revealed in the flesh and to believe in Him.

The first words of Jesus that are recorded in John are not a statement or declaration but a question. Jesus is always more prone to ask questions than to give answers which is a purposeful tactic of His ministry. Jesus asks the two disciples that are following him "What do you seek?" (1:38 NASB). This is a question that Jesus will employ in key interactions that will be revealing the reality of man and their desire toward God. Remember that He didn't entrust Himself to man because He knew what was in them (2:24). The reason for the question was not for Him to learn man but for man to be revealed in their desire for relationship with

God. He asked Mary the same question at the empty tomb (20:15). The disciples desired to know where he was staying so they could stay with him. Jesus' response to the disciples was an invitational promise to come and that they would see (1:39). Mary's desire was to have the body of Jesus to which Jesus responds calling her by name and telling her about his ascension to their Father and God (20:16-17). The other time that Jesus asks the question is in His interaction with Judas, which we will address later. For Jesus to ask this question in John is somewhat of a paradox because Jesus also says some will seek Him but not find Him, and that where He goes, they cannot come (7:34, 8:21, 13:33). This is a picture of that heavenly and earthly relational dynamic that John is revealing to us in the face of the eagle.

The one verse in John that is best known, John 3:16, is nested in a beautiful picture of the face of the eagle. This is a perfect example of the key to the eagle and the themes that the eagle reveals. The context is Jesus answering Nicodemus' questions concerning being born from above. Jesus' response is:

> "Verily, verily, I say unto thee, We speak that we do know, and testify that we have seen; and ye receive not our witness. If I have told you earthly things, and ye believe not, how shall ye believe, if I tell you of heavenly things? And no man hath ascended up to heaven, but he that came down from heaven, even the Son of man which is in heaven. And as Moses lifted up the serpent in the wilderness, even so must the Son of man be lifted up: That whosoever believeth in him should not perish, but have eternal life. For God so loved the world, that he gave his only begotten Son, that

whosoever believeth in him should not perish, but have everlasting life. For God sent not his Son into the world to condemn the world; but that the world through him might be saved. He that believeth on him is not condemned: but he that believeth not is condemned already, because he hath not believed in the name of the only begotten Son of God. And this is the condemnation, that light is come into the world, and men loved darkness rather than light, because their deeds were evil. For every one that doeth evil hateth the light, neither cometh to the light, lest his deeds should be reproved. But he that doeth truth cometh to the light, that his deeds may be made manifest, that they are wrought in God" (3:11-21 KJV).

Read that again carefully and slowly and you can find so many points that could be expounded on. Here are some questions and points to illustrate the eagle: Who is the "we" that is speaking and testifying? There is a telling of earthly and heavenly things dependent upon believing. How is the Son of Man in heaven yet is also the one talking to them, that will be lifted up as Moses lifted up the serpent? God loved the world giving the only begotten Son so those who believe would have eternal life. Practitioners of truth come to the Light so that their deeds are manifest coming from in God. Jesus is also identified by the titles of Son of Man, only begotten Son, Son, Son of God, and the Light. I reckon the way of the eagle in the sky is hard to understand, but don't be discouraged. God loves us and asks that we would believe, even if something is hard to understand. God is patient and desires to fully reveal Himself to us as we walk in relationship together.

Unique to John are two groups of seven. The first group is the 7 "I am" statements. The "I am" statements are Jesus revealing the full connection of divinity and humanity in Himself. The name that God gave to Moses to share with Israel is "I Am" (Exodus 3:14). The name "I Am" could be written about unendingly, but I will suffice to give you the list trusting the Lord will reveal Himself to you as you engage His face. Jesus says, "I Am the Bread of Life" (6:35), the "Light of the world" (8:12), the "Door" (10:9), the "Good Shepherd" (10:11), the "Resurrection and the Life" (11:25), the "Way the Truth the Life" (14:6), and the "Vine" (15:5). The second group of 7 are the signs that Jesus preformed. I refer to the signs by the stories in which they are found. They are the wedding miracle of Cana (2:1-11), the healing of the official's son (4:46-54), the man at the pool of Bethesda (5:1-15), the multiplication of loaves at Passover (6:1-13), walking on water (6:15-21), healing the man born blind (9:1-7), and the raising of Lazarus (11:1-46).

There is no temptation of Jesus in John's gospel because God cannot be tempted (James 1:13). The revealing of Jesus as God is also confirmed in the garden scene of Jesus' arrest. Jesus does not go away to pray and there is not any indication of agony. Jesus fully knows what is going to happen and He is in charge of the scene playing out (18:1). On the cross, Jesus is very much in charge and conscious of fulfilling the scriptures. He tells his mother, "Woman behold your son" and His beloved disciple, "behold your mother" (19:26-27). Then He, to fulfill scripture said, "I am thirsty" and "It is finished" bowing his head and giving up His spirit (19:28-30). The portrayal of Jesus as the eagle is the reality that God is always in control and the eyes of the eagle does not look from the earthly perspective. During trial, tribulation, and crucifixion humanity and divinity are never separate. The eagle still flies even when crucified.

Judas

Dealing with the betrayer and betrayal in John keeps in the theme of seeing from the heavenly perspective and then seeing how it plays out in the earthly. John reveals the most information on the workings of the forces of evil that are playing out. John tells of Jesus asserting Himself amongst the 12 disciples after Peter has confessed that they believe that He is the Holy One of God. Jesus responds with a typical Jesus question that makes a statement. He says, "Have not I chosen you twelve, and one of you is a devil?" (6:70). Judas is identified to the reader as being a devil. It is an important distinction to make here that he is identified as a devil not the devil. We get more information during the supper before the Feast of Passover that the devil had put into the heart of Judas to betray Jesus (13:2). After washing the disciples' feet Jesus reveals more of His knowledge by sharing that He knows one of the twelve will betray Him and that it is Judas to whom He gives a morsel. "And after the sop Satan entered into him. Then said Jesus unto him, That thou doest, do quickly" (13:27 KJV). John is showing that even though earthly things are playing out, Jesus is still above the situation and dictating the steps of the enemy in His midst. When Judas and the Romans come to arrest Jesus in the garden it is Jesus who initiates the interaction. Jesus goes forth, knowing all things that were coming, and asks the question of, "whom do you seek?". They respond that they are looking for "Jesus the Nazarene" and Jesus responds with, "I am" (18:4-5). The same dialogue is repeated, "whom do you seek", "Jesus the Nazarene", and "I am".

The way that the eagle deals with the betrayer is to continue to see from the heavenly perspective. Seeing from the heavenly perspective allows the eagle to confront the betrayer so that the spiritual enemy is seen and is subject to God's plan being accomplished. In the midst of betrayal there is an affirmation of the Godly identity. The eagle should remain true to the calling of God from the beginning. To become flesh and dwell among the people revealing God, I Am, in every situation is the face of the flying eagle.

Redemptive Woman

The redemptive woman for the eagle is Bathsheba. Bathsheba's story is found in 2 Samuel 11, 12. Bathsheba is the wife of Uriah, whose name means, "YHVH is my light". Uriah is not forgotten even though David had him killed so that he could have Bathsheba as his wife. Uriah was faithful to David when David was disloyal to him, ordering him to be put on the frontline of battle to die (11:15). Bathsheba was also the granddaughter of Ahithophel, who was the counselor that betrayed David by counseling Absalom on how to overthrow David. After David had relations with Bathsheba, she purified herself, went home, and then revealed that she was pregnant. After Uriah died in battle David brought Bathsheba into his house and took her as his wife (11:26-27). The child that she bore him died. Bathsheba then bore David another son named Solomon (12:15-25). When David is about to die, Nathan, the prophet, worked with Bathsheba to ensure that Solomon would be enthroned as the next king of Israel (1 Kings 1:11-

53). Bathsheba births the king that comes to be known as the wisest man in the earth. It is also Solomon who builds the temple of the Lord connecting heaven and earth. This was redeeming to David because he was not allowed to build a house for the Lord because of the blood on his hands (1 Chronicles 22:8-10). After David dies it is Solomon who enthrones Bathsheba at his right hand (1 Kings 2:19).

Bathsheba reveals redemption through sonship. It is Bathsheba's perseverance that allows her to birth a son, fight for him, rule with him, and see her son be the wisest man in the earth that builds a house for the Lord to dwell in. When the eagle gets off course it is redemption through sonship that brings forth the prosperity of the people of God and the dwelling of God being among his people. These are the themes that Jesus is identified with in John, the Son of God, Son of Man, the only begotten of God. The Son in which heaven and earth are fully connected. If those who have the face of the eagle get off course, it is through sonship that redemption comes fulfilling the calling of God as seen through Bathsheba.

End of the Gospel

John begins his conclusion with a direct expression of his purpose of writing his gospel. "And many other signs truly did Jesus in the presence of his disciples, which are not written in this book: But these are written, that ye might believe that Jesus is the Christ, the Son of God; and that believing ye might have life through his name" (20:30-31). The whole purpose is for us to believe – and in believing – we may have life. John's statement of his purpose is prefaced with Jesus' statement to Thomas that those who believe even though they have not seen are blessed. The last chapter of John is the story of Jesus making his third appearance after the resurrection at the Sea of Galilee (21:14). The disciples led by Peter, decided to return to the trade that they knew when Jesus called them which was fishing. While the disciples are fishing Jesus appears on the beach and calls out to them telling them their condition of not having caught any fish. He calls them children and tells them to cast their net on the right side of the boat. They obey, even though they could be offended, due to the fact they are being told in their expertise that they are children and how to fish. In their obedience, they catch a great haul of fish. In this dialogue, the beloved disciple recognizes that it is the Lord who is directing them and tells Peter who it is. Peter then throws himself into the sea to get to the Lord quickly with the other disciples coming in the boat with the net of fish. Arriving on the shore, they see a charcoal fire with fish and bread already prepared. Jesus instructs them to bring some of the 153 fish that they have caught. Jesus then has a dialogue with Peter asking three times "do you love me?", with three commands of "tend My lambs," "shepherd My sheep," "tend My sheep." This is the only direct commission outside of Jesus saying, "Peace be unto you: as my Father hath sent me, even so send I you. And when he had said this, he breathed on them, and saith unto them, Receive ye the Holy Ghost: Whose soever sins ye remit, they are remitted unto them; and whose soever sins ye retain, they are retained" (20:21-23). There is a lot in these interactions of Jesus with His disciples and it is only compounded by the fact that John adds that his writings are a limited selection of all that Jesus has done and said (21:25).

The commission of John isn't as clear as his purpose for writing, but the key parts of the commission are peace, receive the Holy Spirit, believe, and follow the Lord. These keys are what allow us to be directed by the unknown Lord until we recognize Him in His resurrection. This is what is seen in the story of catching the 153 fish. The disciples were in a position of not knowing what to do and decided to return to what they did when Jesus found them. Being in a position of our normal work we will be challenged to be humble, willing to listen, and believe that the Lord can instruct us even when we don't know that it is Him. We can believe. We can follow Him. It is our choice and our commission. This is the face of God, the eagle, and when we see Him, we shall be like Him.

CHAPTER 11

THE FOUR FACES

IN LEADERSHIP

W
e are all affected by leadership. Even though we claim equality, we organize ourselves and our world in structures of beliefs and values. This structuring of ourselves and our world requires leadership. One could argue that in anarchy there is still leadership. It may not be seen in a specific leader, but the anarchists are still led. Those who confess that they don't or can't believe in God don't escape leadership either. Those who claim to be the leader of their own lives are subject to being led by something. I believe that God created reality in this way because it is His intrinsic nature. God eternal, the supreme leader of all, and the one who has the only viable claim to not being subject to leadership, is in relationship of oneness in the trinity. God is relational and communal. Relationships and community require leadership, so leadership permeates all creation.

The three listings of the four faces that we saw earlier are all found in connection with the throne of God. In the two mentions in Ezekiel the four living beings/cherubim are under the expanse that is like crystal (1:22,26 10:1).

Then, on top of the expanse is something like a throne (1:26, 10:1). The mention in the book of Revelation has the four living creatures on top of the "sea of glass, like crystal," around and in the middle of the throne (4:6). Also, you have the ark of the covenant that had the cherubim on its cover, which is also called the mercy seat (Ex. 25:18). It is between the cherubim that God speaks to Moses (Exodus 25:22, Number 7:89). These four faces are always connected to the functioning of God's leadership from His throne.

In our personal lives, these four faces help us to lead in different situations that we face. As individuals, we can carry each of these faces and see the impacts of their radiance in our lives. On an individual basis, these faces won't be as developed with specificity that is honed into fullness. When it comes to interacting within a community our leadership role will become more defined and specific. The community setting allows for the furtherance of our growth because the face of a man sharpens the face of another. In the communal setting, we will have one face that is more of our primary identity. The expression of one face in the communal setting allows for the development of the community in direct relation to the development of an individual. When we don't have to have all the answers or perspectives there is a safety, strength, and vitality that we benefit from. In the community, there is going to have to be a true development of each face. This is where the section about confrontation is applied.

The interaction of each face plays out in a dynamic that is unique to each relationship. If you were to place the four faces at the four cardinal directions you would get the lion in the east, the ox in the south, the man in the west, and the eagle in the north. The interaction that is directly across is going to be more confrontational. The eagle and the ox will conflict more directly, and the lion and the man will conflict more directly. There will also be greater protection based on that opposite alignment. The ox and eagle will help each other in their challenges, and the man and lion will help each other in their challenges. If you think about the keys and challenges for each face, we can see the intensity of either protection or conflict that could manifest as each face interacts with the other.

Take for example the man and the lion. The man's key is about relationship, detail, loyalty, the exact story, key relationships, and the lion's challenge is about not competing with the earthly kingdoms. The man has a strength to help the lion identify his people and know which people to focus on. The lion's key is about establishing that reality of kingship and the kingly perspective and the man's challenge is dealing with the weakness of men needing to know how. The lion has a strength that will help the man to deal properly with men so that God's kingdom is established. We can also parallel the lesser images that each one has and how the opposite face will overcome that lesser glory. The lion overcomes the four-footed beast, man's fallen image. The ox overcomes the crawling creature, the eagle's fallen image. The man overcomes the corruptible man, the lion's fallen image. The eagle overcomes the birds, the ox's fallen image. The dynamics of each face's interaction could be specified in greater detail but there wouldn't be enough room in this book.

These four faces are God's design, and as leadership is experienced, we can see His design impacting the variations that we create. Maybe you are familiar with what some have called the four temperaments or some other labeling of the four basic descriptions of personality types. The four temperaments parallel directly the four faces. The lion is the choleric temperament. The ox is the sanguine temperament. The man is the phlegmatic temperament. The eagle is the melancholy temperament. There are other personality assessments for team building and leadership traits. The CIA has an animal model for a team. The four animals that the CIA give are the lion, fox, cheetah, and bear. There animals would parallel lion to lion, fox to eagle, cheetah to ox, and bear to man. They assert that to have a great team you need each of these animals and the traits that they execute. John Trent and Gary Smalley wrote a book called *The Two Sides of Love*. In the book, they identify four personality types represented by animals. Their animals are the lion, otter, golden retriever, and beaver, which parallel the lion, ox, man, and eagle. There are other people that have collected their own group of four animals to exemplify these truths of the four faces. All of these animals, temperament, and personality types can all be traced back to these four faces of the gospels.

In leadership all four of these faces are important. A team that has each of these faces and understands the interworking is better equipped in their mission and purpose. All four of them together provide protection and a capacity to handle situations that may arise. The four faces create a structure of power and authority that is greater than just one face can present on its own. There is a synergy that is experienced by having all four of the faces working together to tell the story or accomplish the mission of the team. This is a revealing of divine synergy in our lives that witnesses of something beyond our human functional capacity.

In our culture the structure of the four can be seen. Consider these famous bands: The Beatles, Led Zepplin, Queen, The Who, Metallica, Van Halen, Kiss, The Doors, The Beach Boys, and The Rolling Stones. It is also seen in our forms of entertainment such as: the Seinfeld characters, the Wizard of Oz, South Park, The A-Team, the hobbits of The Lord of the Rings, Ghost Busters, siblings of Narnia, King of the Hill, Ninja Turtles, The Flintstones, The Golden Girls, schools of Hogwarts, and the Fantastic Four. In the USA we have four presidents carved into Mount Rushmore. I am not claiming that you could peg all of these people into a specific face. I am showing how this structure of four can powerfully play out in aspects of those who we follow or are impacted by. In a negative sense this reality of the four faces can be used to cause destruction. When we, myself and the three men I work with, first started to see this revelation of the four faces of God we saw how it could be negative.

My friend Josh Jordan was studying the rise of Hitler and the Nazi Party for a screenplay that he was writing. As he studied and we were discussing it we found that this structure of four could be seen in its leadership. Studying this time of German leadership, world conflict and seeing how it imploded we could see the destruction that these faces can cause also. The four men that were leaders in the Nazi Party were Adolf Hitler, Joseph Goebbels, Hermann Goering, and Heinrich Himmler. Adolf Hitler was the leader, and he paralleled the lion. Remember that the lion falls to the image of the corruptible man. Hitler was obsessed with being the perfect man and the power of man's kingdom ruling. Joseph Goebbels (ox) was the chief propagandist and communication director. He plowed the fields of Germany so that the message of the Nazi party could be planted. He took on the fallen image of the bird in his false messaging of intellectualism. Hermann Goering (man) was a fighter pilot ace and war hero that led the Luftwaffe and reformed a lot of the military. He developed the four-year plan to dig Germany out of its economic hole. Goering was described as charming and moved in the circles of social elites. His fallen image was to the beast to power the military and restart the German economy. Heinrich Himmler (eagle) led the SS for the Nazi party. He was involved in occult practices, symbolism, and collected relics and art of occultism. He was the organizer of the concentration and work camps that facilitated the death of so many people. That is a picture of people being brought into the place where they would be killed like the fallen image of the crawling creature. These four men encapsulate the power of how these four faces can work together in a negative way. Their working together was not on equal terms and Hitler was the main leader. These four men operated in a way that released a throne and authority of destruction, because of their pride and deception. It would be interesting to consider how these men could have had a good impact if they could have had a relationship with God that would have transformed them to carry the identities of the lion, ox, man, and eagle.

Leadership is developed in the crucible of choices we make. Will we turn our face to God or to ourselves? We are beholding the faces of those who will be the leaders of tomorrow. What does our face reveal to them? God has designed us to be leaders. Are we leaders that have healthy relationships that bear forth life? Ask yourself what face you have, and what face the leaders in your life have. Identifying the face of the leaders in your life will create an opportunity for you to communicate and interact with them more efficiently and effectively. As you begin to identify your face and others, remember that leaders are not made in an instant. Leadership requires maturity and maturing is a process. The development of your face is a process. The more you step into the leadership roles you have, no matter how big or small, the more your face will be seen with clarity. It is a process. In your personal life, you can probably identify aspects of each face, but as you step into a role of leadership on a larger scale you will find yourself established in one face.

To conclude this chapter, I am going to give you some identifiers for each face to help you start to think about the leaders in your life. I want you to remember that these identifiers are not a cookie-cutter shape that you can apply to someone, or they must fit exactly. There are other factors such as life experiences, motivational gifting, life circumstances and stresses, that should be considered. Remember that it is about face-to-face relationships, not about defining someone that you won't engage face-to-face. These are all positive identifiers. The negative identifiers would be based on the lesser image of glory for each face.

The Lion: Kingdom/Domain Focused, Territorial, Protective, Authoritative, Structured, Bold, Assertive, Directive, Standard Oriented, Take Charge, Firm, Opinionated, Definitive, Establish Framework, and Identify People that Belong. Negatively the Corrupt

Man.

The Ox: Service Focused, Sacrificial, Work Oriented, Driven, Fast Paced, Urgent, High Energy, Achievements and Results Oriented, Pursuant, Motivated, At Least Do Something Mentality, Creative, Optimistic, Strong Willed, Disciplined, Active, Rest and Have Fun so they can Work More, Communicative, Inspire Others to Work, Now Focused, Hidden Spiritual Side, and Burden Bearer. Negatively the Bird.

The Man: Relational, People Focused, Connective, Thoughtful, Tolerant, Patient, Facts and Integrity Oriented, Interpersonal, Empathetic, Story Tellers, Nurturing, Loyal, Understanding, Even Keeled, Joy, Unifying, Welcoming, Sensitive to People and Circumstances, Humane, and Inclusive. Negatively the Four-Footed Beast.

The Eagle: Visionary, Creative, Incarnational Focused, Deliberate, Specific, Precise, Persistent, Reserved, Analytical, Agile, Shrewd, Ingenuity, Strategic, Innovative, Sneaky, Efficient, Adaptable, Perceptive, Inquisitive, Long-Term Perspective, and Reserved until Specific Things are Perceived. Negatively the Creeping or Crawling Creature.

CHAPTER 12

HAVE A FACE,

GET A FACE

G od has a face. Do you? Do you know what you look like? Have you taken any time to intentionally look at yourself? "For God, who said, 'Light shall shine out of darkness,' is the One who has shone in our hearts to give the Light of the knowledge of the glory of God in the face of Christ" (2 Corinthians 4:6 NASB).

Earlier we discussed the story of Cain and how he allowed his countenance to fall. In his story, we saw the role our face plays in the maturing process. Let us once again look at his story with some secondary source information. Jude, in his letter, gives a warning to the unbelieving and those who revile the things they don't understand. He then says that these men "have gone the way of Cain, and for pay, they have given themselves up to the error of Balaam and perished in the rebellion of Korah" (1:11 NASB). This way, error, and perishing is the counterfeit to Jesus who is the Way, the Truth, and the Life (John 14:6). The second piece of secondary information speaking of the comparison of Abel's sacrifice to Cain's, comes from the writer of

Hebrews. He says, "By faith Abel offered to God a better sacrifice than Cain, through which he was attested to be righteous, God testifying about his gifts, and through faith, though he is dead, he still speaks" (Hebrews 11:4 NASB).

What is the way of Cain? Cain's story breaks down into three key moments. Recall from the story in Genesis 4 that Cain brought an offering of the fruit of the ground to God. This first key part shows a lack of faith. The reason that we know this is from the revelation of the author of Hebrews. In Hebrews, the difference between the sacrifice of Cain and Abel is that Abel's sacrifice was by faith. God didn't make a judgement based on what was brought by each one, but His response was based on how they brought their offerings. They both brought the fruit of their occupation. It was Abel that brought his offering by faith. That means that Able made an offering based on the "substance of things hoped for, the evidence of things not seen" (Hebrews 11:1 KJV), which is faith. Cain didn't bring his offering based on the substance of what he was hoping for and what he could not see. "Whatsoever is not of faith is sin" (Romans 14:23b KJV).

The second key part of Cain's story is that he became very angry and let his countenance fall. This second key shows that Cain disconnected himself from the source of his help. Cain gave up hope by turning away from the Lord. Hope is the connection that we have between where we are and where we want to be. When Cain allowed his face to fall downward, he disconnected himself from God, who is our true hope. Hope is the anchor of our souls that hold us anchored in the storms of life and our failures (Hebrews 6:19). The fallen countenance of Cain's face severed him from the anchor that would hold him in relationship with God, and he was blown into the sin that was crouching at the door waiting for him.

The third key part of Cain's story is that Cain revolted against Abel and killed his brother (Genesis 4:8). This action of Cain is the final blow of Cain's way. Cain kills his brother. This was the blow of death to kill the example of what should have been. Cain killed not only his brother but also his opportunity to learn in humility. Cain talked with Abel and told him something. Cain's words and the response of Abel are not recorded in the scriptures. We know that Abel knew of something that made his offering regarded by God. Cain could have desired to learn from Abel what was unseen, and what he had evidence of. Cain could have learned of Abel's faith and maybe seen redemption in his relationship with God. "We know that we have passed from death unto life, because we love the brethren. He that loveth not his brother abideth in death. Whosoever hateth his brother is a murderer: and ye know that no murderer hath eternal life abiding in him. Hereby perceive we the love of God, because he laid down his life for us: and we ought to lay down our lives for the brethren" (1 John 3:13-16 KJV). Cain's way was murder, death, and hate.

The way of Cain is the complete opposite of the way that Jesus is. Cain's way is absent of faith, hope, and love. Cain's way was based on a substance of what he could see in himself, the despair of disconnection, and indifference. Jesus is the way, and He is faith, hope, and love. We are to live by the faith of the Son of God (Galatians 2:20). Our hope is God our Savior, the Lord Jesus Christ (1 Timothy 1:1). We love because he first loved us and laid down his life for us (1 John 4:19, John 15:13). The face of Jesus reveals the way, the truth, and the life that He is. We can look unto the face of God and see the face of Jesus that transforms us into the way full of faith hope and love.

Humility – humility is key to us having and receiving a face. Don't be afraid to let go of your masks. "But we all, with open face beholding as in a glass the glory of the Lord, are changed into the same image from glory to glory, even as by the Spirit of the Lord" (2 Corinthians 3:18 KJV). Allow yourself to take some time to look unto God's face. This is transformation. It might be scary, like looking into the unknown, knowing that it is beyond you, but that is okay. If we wrestle with God and lose, we will still be better off seeing His face and losing because He will transform us.

Remember that having genuine relationship means to be face-to-face. The perfect comes and the partial is done away with as we are face-to-face with God and others. Love is the perfect that comes as we are willing to be face-to-face, knowing fully as we are fully known. There are a lot of good things that are partial. Don't settle for the partial, knowing that there is more for you. The perfect, the complete is for you. The greatest is love. Love stands face-to-face and transforms all. Our greatest choice and our greatest opportunity in life is to face God, ourselves, and each other.

CONCLUSION

A s this book concludes, there are a couple of reminders that I want to leave with you. First, this book is not a complete exposition of the gospels, by intent. There is much more to the story of Jesus than what any one person could write in a book. Relationships are an adventure. Love is an adventure. We have the opportunity of this adventure with God and others. This book is a beginning or a continuation for you. This book is so that you will be stimulated in your relationship with God, that you would engage His face and be transformed. Take this book and expound on it. Seek God and His face. Receive the revelation that life doesn't have to be lived with a covered face. You can see God face to face. Take the risk. Have a face. Let your light shine.

We are all searching for that way to the tree of life. Remember that when man was driven from the garden, God placed cherubim with a flaming sword to guard the way to the tree of life. The only way to partake of the Tree of Life is to face and engage the cherubim who carry the four faces of God. God has made a way for us to eat of the Tree of Life. That way is through the blood and body of Jesus Christ who loves us and laid down his life for us. It is his face through the four faces by which we behold God's face. Adam and Eve hid themselves in the garden. You no longer have to hide yourself. In the Spirit of the Lord, you are free. God desires for you to see his face and engage Him.

Be reminded that there is much more to life than the temporal that you see around you. Remember that in the face of God, there is fullness of joy. Don't give up. Don't quit on yourself and your heart. There is abundant hope in God. With His face, you are an overcomer being transformed into His image from glory to glory. Be clothed with your heavenly identity in Christ.

I pray that as you have read this book that you would be encouraged to have a face, to engage God's face, to be humble and seek God's face continually, and to be transformed into that same image of glory that He desires for you to be. I pray that the Lord bless you and keep you; the Lord make His face shine on you and be gracious to you; the Lord lift up His countenance on you and give you peace. I pray that you will know the only true God and Jesus Christ whom He has sent for this is eternal life. I pray that you will know that the Son of God has come and given us an understanding that we may know Him that is true, and we are in His Son Jesus Christ. Life and Peace to you. Amen.

ACKNOWLEDGEMENTS

First, I want to thank God who has been merciful and gracious to me, especially while writing this book. It has been His relationship of revelation that has led me to experience what is written on these pages.

I want to thank Melchizedek Christian Church who has been an encouragement and support. Thank you for your prayers.

I want to thank those who helped edit this book so that it would be better for all those who read it after you.

I want to thank Chloe Emmerling who helped with cover design ideas and some original sketches.

Lastly, I want to acknowledge Don Crossland, Joshua Jordan, and Joshua Prior who have been the friends whose faces have sharpened my own. Thank you for all the times of discourse and fellowship in the things of God.

BIBLIOGRAPHY

Hill, C.E. *Who Chose the Gospels.* New York, NY, Oxford University Press, 2012.

Bullinger, E.W. *Number in Scripture.* Grand Rapids, MI, Kregel Publications, 1967.

GET INVOLVED

Did you like the book?

Did you find it helpful?

Let the world know!

Authors in today's world are more dependent on the reader than ever before. You and others like you are the momentum behind a good book. You can help get this book into more reader's hands!

Please review the book on Amazon, Goodreads and anywhere else people discuss the books they have read. Reviews are a huge help to the author and others. There is no such thing as too many reviews.

Post on any of your social media about the book and how you found it useful in your life. Tell your friends and family about it.

If you would like to contact the author, you can send an email to daniel.prior110@outlook.com.

ABOUT THE AUTHOR

Daniel Prior was born and raised around Nashville, TN. He earned his bachelor's degree in Plant and Soil Science from Middle Tennessee State University in 2014. His love of watching and seeing the growth in people and creation was engendered at a younger age as he helped manage a landscaping company. Even though he was a Christian from a young age, he was thrust into a deeper relationship with Jesus while encountering Christ in a most personal way in college. A disciple of Don Crossland for many years, an esteemed Father of the Faith, he was spurred on in his relationship with Jesus Christ ever coming more and more into communion with His Heavenly Father. He was then ordained into the Ministry at Melchizedek Christian Church in the year 2012.

His favorite author, G. K. Chesterton said, "The true object of all human life is play. Earth is a task garden; heaven is a playground." This is exactly who Daniel is, realizing that a good farmer plants, watches, and harvests. But with all good work comes great play. The reality of heavenly things and the most important, the risen Christ, continues to be a fuel for understanding and encouragement in growing in the faith. After all the praying, reading, listening and studying through the last years, His voice continually utters John 17:3, "And this is eternal life, that they may know You, the only true God, and Jesus Christ whom You have sent." (NASB)

	Matthew (Lion)	Mark (Ox)	Luke (Man)	John (Eagle)
General Description	King, Kingdom	Sacrificial Servant of God	Man, Humanity, Relationship	Eternity, Divinity, Heavenly to Earthly
Key	True King for people of the kingdom	Get to work, Prayer time with the Father	Detail, Order, Truth, Relational Integrity	Become flesh Dwell among the people
Challenge	Not fight the Earthly Kingdoms	Maintain Prayer so not overworked by demands of others	Weak Belief, having to know how	Overcome Skepticism, Unbelief
Lesser Image	Corruptible Man	Bird	Four Footed Beast	Crawling Creature
How to Confront	Call to right battles and battlefields, refocus on the kingdom	Call to right yoke, be direct, give space to kick and jump around	Call to relationship, show how, facts, intention	Call to incarnation, present need
Genealogy	Kingly, Abraham and David	None, work of Isaiah and John	Humanity all the way to Adam	None, Eternal Beginning
Judas	Count Costs of kingdom and actions	No response, keep serving	See the how of betrayal, confront the how not the person, See outside influence	See from heavenly perspective and God's plan in the midst of it
Redemptive Woman	Tamar, Redeem through Authority	Rahab, Redeem through Sacrifice	Ruth, Redeem through Relationship	Bathsheba, Redeem through Sonship

SeraphCreative

Heaven's Heart for Earth

Seraph Creative is a collective of artists, writers, theologians & illustrators who desire to see the body of Christ grow into full maturity, walking in their inheritance as Sons Of God on the Earth.

Sign up to our newsletter to know about the release of the next book in the series, as well as other exciting releases.

Visit our website :
www.seraphcreative.org

www.ingramcontent.com/pod-product-compliance
Lightning Source LLC
Chambersburg PA
CBHW051204120626
46547CB00013B/1199